| | |
|---|---|
| How to use this Guide | 5 |
| Introduction | 6 |
| Day 1: 20th September | 7 |
| Day 2: 21st September | 9 |
| Day 3: 22nd September | 12 |
| Day 4: 24th September | 18 |
| Day 5: 24th September | 26 |
| Day 6: 25th September | 31 |
| Day 7: 26th September | 40 |
| Day 8: 27th September | 45 |
| Day 9: 28th September | 51 |
| Day 10: 29th September | 55 |
| Day 11: 30th September | 62 |
| Day 12: 1st October | 68 |
| Day 13: 2nd October | 75 |
| Day 14: 3rd October | 82 |
| Day 15: 4th October | 88 |
| Day 16: 5th October | 95 |
| Day 17: 6th October | 100 |
| Day 18: 7th October | 104 |
| Day 19: 8th October | 112 |
| Day 20: 9th October | 118 |
| Day 21: 10th October | 121 |
| Day 22: 11th October | 126 |
| Day 23: 12th October | 131 |
| Day 24: 13th October | 138 |
| Day 25: 14th October | 142 |
| Day 26: 15th October | 148 |
| Day 27: 16th October | 152 |
| Day 28: 17th October | 159 |
| Day 29: 18th October | 162 |

Day 30: 19th October .................................................................................................................. 168
Day 31: 20th October .................................................................................................................. 174
The Interactive Route .................................................................................................................. 175
Quick Itinerary ............................................................................................................................ 176
    Day 1: Penrith ........................................................................................................................ 176
    Day 2: Beacon Hill Monument, Gareloch, Gare loch .............................................................. 176
    Day 3: Succoth, the Cobbler Hike, Loch Eck ........................................................................... 176
    Day 4: Loch Eck, Puck's Glen, Loch Earn ................................................................................ 176
    Day 5: Loch Earn, Ben Vorlich Hike ....................................................................................... 177
    Day 6: Perth, The Hermitage .................................................................................................. 177
    Day 7: A'Chaileach hike, Newtonmore ................................................................................... 177
    Day 8: Ruthven Barracks, Falls of Foyer, Loch Ness ................................................................ 177
    Day 9: Laundry, Rosemarkie, Chanonry Point, Brora Beach ................................................... 178
    Day 10: Forsinard Tower, Forsinain Trail, Sandside Bay Beach .............................................. 178
    Day 11: John O'Groats, Duncansby Stacks, Dunnet Head, Castletown Beach ........................ 178
    Day 12: Achininver Beach, Moine House ............................................................................... 178
    Day 13: Ceannabeinne Beach, Smoo Cave, Balnakeil Beach, Kyle of Durness ....................... 179
    Day 14: Balnakeil Beach, Smoo Cave, Culkein Road ............................................................. 179
    Day 15: Stoer Lighthouse, Little Assynt, Ardveck Castle, Ullapool .......................................... 179
    Day 16: Corrishalloch Gorge, Ardessie Falls, Little Loch Broom .............................................. 179
    Day 17: Gairloch Beach, Gairloch Harbour, Applecross Sands ............................................. 180
    Day 18: AppleCross Pass, Bheinn Bhan, Plockton Airfield ..................................................... 180
    Day 19: Plockton Coral beach, Sligachan Old Bridge, Eas a 'Bhradain Falls, Rigg viewpoint .... 180
    Day 20: Talisker Distillery, Eyenort River ................................................................................. 180
    Day 21: Old Man of Storr, Kilt Rock, Mealt Falls, An Corran Beach ....................................... 181
    Day 22: Uig, The Fairy Glen, Loch Scavaig ........................................................................... 181
    Day 23: Bla Bheinn hike, Rigg viewpoint ................................................................................ 181
    Day 24: Quiraing, Plockton .................................................................................................... 181
    Day 25: Camusdarach Beach, Arisaig .................................................................................... 182
    Day 26: Arisaig, Glen Nevis Holiday Park, Inchree Falls ........................................................ 182
    Day 27: Inchree Falls, Steall Waterfalls ................................................................................... 182
    Day 28: Blarmacfoldach viewpoint, Achintee Road ................................................................ 182
    Day 29: Ben Nevis, Seagull Island ......................................................................................... 183
    Day 30: Glencoe, Glen Etive, Kilchurn Castle, Falls of Falloch, Milarrochy Bay ...................... 183
    Bonus Tracks .......................................................................................................................... 184
The Hills and Hikes ..................................................................................................................... 185
    Day 3: The Cobbler ................................................................................................................ 185
    Day 5: Ben Vorlich ................................................................................................................. 185

Day 7: A'Chailleach, Cairngorms ...................................................................................................185
Day 18: Beinn Bhan..........................................................................................................................185
Day 23: Bla Bheinn ..........................................................................................................................186
Day 29: Ben Nevis ............................................................................................................................186

As documented by

Kath Cross

and

Stuart Hall

## How to use this Guide

- Enjoy our story and photographs.

- Refer to the Quick Itinerary and Interactive route to find locations

- Scan the QR codes using your phone's camera to watch our feature videos on locations in the itinerary

- Scan the QR codes in the Hills section for detailed walking routes

- Use the blank sections at the back to plan your own Scottish adventure

- Pop this guide in your rucksack, suitcase, or bag and use it to refer to en route

- Show us your adventure on social media and hashtag #vanavigation

- Recommend us to a friend/Leave an Amazon review!

# Introduction

It's the summer of 2022 and thanks to some sensational squirrelling of funds by my rather clever boyfriend and my ability to work on the road, it's finally happening! This coming Autumn we're off on a Scottish roadtrip in his trusty Mercedes Sprinter, set up for offgrid living. All that's left to do is plan the trip.

The obvious plan is to do the NC500 in late summer but it's become very popular, so we decide we'll mix up the route, add in some other places, and cut out chunks of the NC500. We end up planning for Autumn in the hope it'll be a little quieter than the summer and we'll get to experience the changing seasons. If we're really lucky we'll get to see late summer sun for the beaches, changing leaves in the forests, and maybe we'll even be lucky enough to see a pair of rutting stags, and catch the first snow on the hills too. Who knows what to expect?

We leave the route-planning to fate by researching some good days out in Scotland, tagging them all on Google maps and making no route at all. We're going to wing it day by day and see how many of the places we've tagged we can get in. What could possibly go wrong? *

*In fact, nothing went very wrong for the whole trip. If you're reading this in hope of a disastrous travelogue full of funny but excruciating stories about getting stuck in the mud, burned out clutches, or being stranded in Scotland, you'll be disappointed. If you're hoping for a fun adventure read and some inspiration for your own trip, well, we hope you like our story.

Here are our thirty days in Scotland. A travel guide in story form.

Come with us!

## Day 1: 20th September

Let's see how living in a tiny space together for four weeks goes. We always talk about how big Stuart's van is compared to mine. It's an XLWB Jumbo Sprinter and makes my VW Transporter look like a toy, but make no mistakes, living in a van is a tiny space and requires a certain mindset. We spend all our spare time in the van and we've holidayed together but this will be our longest trip yet, more than four weeks.

Stuart has already filled the tank with diesel, topped up the LPG and grabbed some groceries (I haven't looked yet but I'd bet it's snack heavy!), so all that is left to do is pack the van. As I try and fit my stuff into the van, and Stuart mutters about the legal weight, I chuckle internally thinking how this small space mindset needs to kick in quickly.

Even with the most inventive packing in the world, packing light for four weeks during changing seasons for two adults and a dog is not easy, and presents its own challenges even before we're on the road.

After what seems like an age, my van is safely parked up off road for a month, Stuart's van is packed and we're ready to hit the road! With our lackadaisical planning, we don't have any route. So far, we have just one stop-off planned, Beacon Hill Monument in Cumbria. We choose this because It's picturesque, it offers a nice walk for the morning, and it's less than a 5-minute drive from Junction 38 on the M6. Really, it's just a quick overnight stop-off and we're planning to push through to the Scottish border in the morning.

As a writer and freelancer, I work on the road. My laptop is a constant feature of our travels and I work in all the dead spaces, so I take the long motorway run as a chance to get a little ahead with work stuff so I can enjoy a few days work-free as we get over the border.

There's not much to say about the journey really, we make good time, the dog is impeccably behaved, and even with the rush-hour through the Midlands, it's uneventful. There's some good-natured excitement as we get further north, and we chat and snack on the road. By the time we finally arrive at the base of the hill where the Beacon Hill Monument stands, it's late and the light of the day is disappearing fast. Thanks to a quick Burger King at the services, there's nothing to do and no cooking so we head out to look at the night sky.

It's beautiful here. It's far too dark to see the landscape but with no light pollution in any direction and not a single street light, the night sky illuminates our gravel park up beautifully. There's the slightest slither of a moon, about a quarter of the surface as it wanes and this means the stars appear even brighter than usual. As I lean back against the cold metal of the van and relax my eyes, allowing them to adjust to the darkness, the whole Milky Way appears streaked across the sky, an otherworldly light-show beating any fireworks display.

Time for bed. Tomorrow we'll be in Scotland!

## Day 2: 21st September

It was dark here when we arrived last night, and at new park ups there's always the sense of anticipation for the surroundings when you wake up. Today did not disappoint.

The Lake District in Cumbria is one of the most beautiful areas of England, and while we're at one of the less touristy and more understated part of it, it's still remarkably beautiful. The Beacon Hill Monument is at the top of a fell, so there's not too much climbing for us today, but all around are rolling hills and in the distance, the silhouettes of Helvellyn and Blencartha.

After some breakfast we head out for a walk, and as we climb up the hill towards the monument, we both promise ourselves we'll come back to the Lake District to bag some proper hills. It's breathtakingly stunning here and as we walk up the fell, I have a little Bronte moment and can completely understand how some lonely woman could fall in love with a moody antihero, and live in perfect melancholy forever, with this backdrop of bleak moorland and exposed fells.

We bought a drone for the trip and as it's the perfect day for it, we decide to get it up in the air So we can see how good the footage is. We've really been looking forward to getting shots of us two and the dog and then panning out to our environment to show off the Scottish landscapes and give a good view of where we are. Stuart gets out the drone, connects it all up to the GPS, sets off the propellors ready to fly… and the dog goes absolutely bloody mental! Any ideas of cool drone shots of the three of us are quickly forgotten as I try and get Nala under control and stop her eating the drone.

It's lovely here but we're both keen to move on and start our "Scottish road trip" so we start to head back to the van and plan the next day of the trip. A quick spot of lunch and some route planning and we hit the motorway for the remainder of the journey.

As Stuart puts some miles under the wheels, we decide where to go first. A Scottish friend recommended The Cobbler walk to us so we're doing that as our first big Scottish adventure. We plan a route in that direction.

The last leg of motorway, and we see the sign, Welcome to Scotland! I'm not known for being understated, and with all the excitement of a small child seeing the big wheel at the fair, I am hanging out the van window trying to grab a picture of the sign. After a decade of hoping and planning we are finally in Scotland!

This leg of the journey doesn't take too long, yet another fuel stop, and after a quick check on some of our apps, we find a quiet car park on the edge of some woodland called Whistlefield Car Park. We're near a place called Gareloch. Although it's marked as a viewpoint, it's not a match for the magical views we've seen of Scotland in guide books. We made it though, we're in Scotland! The car park has specific motorhome parking, so the bays are nice and long and the car park is flat, which if you travel in a van you'll know is an important detail. We need somewhere to stop and rest and take stock to plan the next couple of days, and this is perfect.

After parking up, we're keen to stretch our legs and the dog really needs some exercise, so we head through the woodland, down towards Gare Loch. The woodlands are pretty - if a little treacherous - as we go downhill. On the way down we discover a dog's grave with a stone marked Cassie, passing walkers have left sticks on top. Judging by the number of sticks, we guess Cassie must have been the 'goodest dog!'.

It's nice to get out and get some fresh air, but we're both a little underwhelmed by the whole area. I find myself hoping the rest of Scotland isn't like this and start wondering whether Scotland is really going to be as picturesque as the travel guides promise.

After returning to the van, we are both exhausted after two days travelling. While Stuart cooks dinner, I check the map, marking off Succoth car park at the head of Loch Long for tomorrow as the start of The Cobbler walk. We grab an early night, excited for our first Scottish hike and mountain, though at 884 metres, The Cobbler is a Corbett rather than a Munro. I consider myself on the experienced side of the hiking scale, but as I drift off to sleep I am apprehensive as I think about walking and navigating hills in an area I am completely unfamiliar with.

# Day 3: 22nd September

After a nice peaceful night's sleep, we're up early preparing for our hike up The Cobbler.

The Cobbler is a rocky Corbett and is an important site for rock climbing in the South Highlands, taking its common name from the outline of the top of the mountain that takes the shape of a Cobbler bent over his last. In the 19th Century it was known as The Cobbler and his Wife, but the shorter name now prevails. On many maps it's marked as Ben Arthur, an anglicisation of the mountain's full Scottish Gaelic name Bheinn Artair. It is part of Arrochar Alps, and is one of Scotland's most popular mountains, despite falling short of Munro height at 884 metres.

From my research I can see that The Cobbler has three summits, the middle being the biggest with a tricky pinnacle. We're heading for the North Summit. Once you get to the prominence of the peak, there are two main routes up, an 'easy' paved route around the back of the peak, or a scramble up the front. Always up for a challenge, we are opting for the scramble up the front, and coming down the rear path.

By the time we've eaten our breakfast and got into our hiking gear, it's gone 10am. It's time to head off and get started. We're worried it'll be busy but as it turns out, the car park, which is at the head of Loch Long is aptly sized and we have plenty of room to park.

After marvelling at how pretty the loch is with the sky reflected on its still surface, we pull on our rucksacks and start the hike. The weather is forecast to be changeable, and we know how hard mountain weather is to predict so we're just hoping we don't get a soaking (spoiler alert, we get a soaking!).

We start on the well-marked path, zigzagging up through the forestry, rewarded at every switchback with more and more dazzling views of Loch Long as we climb. It's steep, but the zig-zagged path is taking some of the strain out of the elevation.

A younger couple passes us, but the day is quiet, and we have not seen many people since we set out. The forestry is full of the invasive Himalayan balsam. I tend to pull it out in the spring, but this has all gone to seed, which is where it spreads. I've recently learned the seedpods are edible if you can catch them before they explode, so we eat them on the ascent, laughing about how we're helping native species and how they taste like garden peas.

As we climb out of the Forestry, a large stream and hydro-dam appears to our left. We clamber down to take some pictures, our usual trick of wandering off-piste to discover things, making every hike distance increase by at least a quarter as we do so. The path has levelled out and the three peaks of the Cobbler are clear now, and daunting! I'm internally cursing my determination for us to take the more technical route up the front.

Climbers have been coming to this area to hone their skills on these rock faces since the late 1800s, and I've seen what women climbers wore back then, if they can do it, we can too!

As we follow the Allt a' Bhalachain upstream along the path, the Narnain Boulders loom as we navigate around them. These massive boulders make us look tiny, patterned with swirly layers and chunks of quartz, they serve as a reminder that things on mountains don't always stay still and why great care must always be taken.

This is a lovely hike so far, and still the prominence rises above us as the valley closes in on either side, narrowing the lower pass through the mountains to a gully.

We're not following that lower path, it's time to start ascending again and eventually we see our left turn, taking us across the Allt a' Bhalachain, leaping stones to keep our feet dry. We start to climb proper, and as daunting as it had appeared from the lower path, there are plenty of rough stone ledges acting as steps, the path is well-walked and erosion marks from hikers before us show us the way. So far the weather is warm, dry and still and as I walk ahead with Nala, Stuart gets the drone out and takes some shots. He catches up with us as we climb through a waterfall, the path becoming a little rougher and less obvious the higher we get.

After a lot more scrambling, we're faced with the large, slightly sloping plateau of wet rock to be navigated before we reach the summit. Across this and it's just one last climb to the top where we find a small cairn marking the large overhang of this unusually shaped peak.

The views from the peak are sensational, you can see across to Beinn Narnain (where the boulders rolled from), to Beinn Ime on the other side, Ben Vorlich to the North (this one is also in our sights) and down to Loch Long. From here it seems there are nothing but mountains and lochs in the world, with peaks rising and falling for as far as the eye can see.

After some drone footage and some silly pictures at the peak, mostly of me standing on small ledges while Stuart has a heart attack, we descend the steps on the North side. Clouds are rolling in, low, dark clouds and soon we're engulfed as the heavens open and we're getting soaked.

That's the last we see of the peak and as we drop below the clouds, The Cobbler remains shrouded for the rest of our walk.

By the time we get back to the Narnain Boulders, we're feeling accomplished, but we're soaked through. Apart from the descent of the prominence down the steps to the North, the return route is the same way as we climbed. We plod along in the drizzle, chatting about how wonderfully varied the hike has been, offering forestry, glen, scramble, and dramatic views from the peak and as we approach the forest once more, we see our first Scottish rainbow.

The zigzags through the forestry feel like they take an age on the way back down and we're both starting to feel the strain of the day. By the time we get back to the van we have used all seven hours parking that we paid for, which isn't surprising as we stop every five minutes to take pictures and like to hang around at the peak once we get there. The Cobbler goes down as one of my favourite mountains, though at this early stage of the trip, who knows what's to come!

We get back to the van and dump our stuff, tired after the hike. It's time to sit and decide on a park up for the night. We're already planning a quieter day tomorrow to rest after the hike. I have some work to catch up with in the morning and then we're planning to spend the afternoon at a nearby place called Puck's Glen. The map shows the Glen at the southern end of Loch Eck, just a few minutes away. After consulting the apps and Google maps, we have a couple of possible park ups for the night along this stretch, so off we go, bellies rumbling to find our home for the night.

Of the park ups, the smallest one on the map, about three quarters of the way down the eastern shore of Loch Eck is empty and allows us to pull up right by the water. Too dark to really appreciate the view, we settle down for the night, Stuart finding the energy to cook us a meal before we shower and fall into bed.

## Day 4: 24th September

We have woken up in the most beautiful place on earth, we're both agreed that it is by far the best park up we have EVER stayed at, and we're only four days into our trip! I am in a great mood this morning. Does it get better than this? We really are living the dream. We are taking photos out of the van window before we even get out of bed.

We found this spot on one of the apps we use and it's tiny, not a carpark, but a small hardstanding nestled into the trees alongside the road. We're far enough off the road for the van not to shake as people drive past, but there was a little traffic noise this morning. You step out of the van steps from the water's edge of Loch Eck, which is where I find Stuart when I drag myself out of bed. He's flying the drone across the water, creating some brilliant footage of the loch and the van. The drone has turned out to be a fun accessory and we'd highly recommend it to anyone who is interested in photography.

The water is perfectly still, creating stunning reflections of the adjoining countryside. On the other side of the loch is more forestry, and above that the peaks of Beinn Bheag to the right, and Beinn Mhor to the left just behind it. The peaks keep appearing and disappearing behind swirling clouds, offering us an ever-changing landscape to spend the morning admiring.

I remember I'm supposed to be working, so I leave Stuart and Nala playing at the water's edge and I sit in the van at my laptop. Nothing makes you more productive than wanting an early finish. No one wants to work on a fun roadtrip, but the job I do allows the very lifestyle we're living and that's enough reason to be disciplined. I've taken the first few days here off work, so I really can't complain, and I am all finished by lunchtime, so I head outside, sit on a rock, and enjoy the delightful view of loch, mountains, and forest that this park up affords.

The water's edge is like a rocky beach, and someone has set up a large stone campfire, although we don't use it. As we sit there it's clear how low the water levels are for this time of year. The whole of the UK has had a dry summer and despite being a very water rich country, you can see this has affected Scotland too. On the shoreline is a huge patch of Michaelmas Daisies growing in a big tuft, their long slender stems displaying lilac coloured, spindly flower heads, bobbing in the breeze. The part of the shoreline they have rooted and grown in will surely be under water in a few short weeks as we move into Autumn.

There aren't many signs of Autumn here yet though, and despite some low cloud swirling across the loch and obscuring the mountains behind, and the odd shower skating across the loch's surface, it's a lovely day that still feels like late summer, the still green broadleaf woodland that surrounded us, agreeing with our findings.

I tidy up the van. A few days travelling and getting settled into the journey equates to a sink full of dishes, every inch of the sofa covered in folded up clothes and the detritus of life. This is the reality of van-living, tidying up a dozen times a day, and moving things from place to place around the van to make room for whatever you're doing at the time. As big as Stuart's van is… relatively, it's still a small space for two of us and a dog. For those doing van life with a family and children, we greatly admire you!

We've planned this park up around a place we want a visit, a nearby glen called Puck's Glen. Puck's Glen is a natural, river formed ravine with a walking trail that has been popular since the Victorian period. The walk follows the Eas Mor stream along a rocky gorge and we are very much looking forward to it. It's after lunch and I'm ravenous, so we hang around a little longer as I throw some scrambled eggs and baguettes together and then we get ready to venture down the road to the Puck's Glen car park.

There are two routes from the car park, up into the woodland, or along a flat tree lined trail. We opt for the flat trail in the hope that when we do start to climb towards the higher part we'll be walking at the waterfalls and not looking back at them.

The tree lined trail is beautiful and boasts some of the biggest evergreens I have ever seen, interspersed with rhododendron, a reminder that this place has been a tourist destination since the Victorian period. Many of these are still producing flowers, despite the lateness of the season, little purple blooms hanging on and defying the Autumn chill.

The first thing we see along this trail is a red squirrel, Nala spotting it first and alerting us. Stuart has never seen a red squirrel and I was about 10 years old the last time I saw one so we're both thrilled! We watch his tiny, nimble frame and bushy tail hop from branch to branch as he escapes the glare of Nala, whose stance indicates prey, and in the blink of an eye he's gone.

We made a little fun wish list before we came of things we'd really love to see while we're here in Scotland. The list is red squirrel, red deer, rutting stags, golden eagle, sea eagle, seals, whales, dolphins, otters, and beavers. That's one thing ticked off and we're only four days in.

After about a kilometre or so we reach the small, picturesque bridge over the Eas Mor, with a sign reading "Puck's Glen" instructing us to turn right along the stream. As we take the path, the sides of the gorge rise on either side of us with every step we take, larch trees balanced precariously on the steep banks towering above us into the sky.

As we follow the path upstream, waterfalls trip over waterfalls to greet us as the river tumbles down its rocky path. The steep banks verdant with mosses, ferns, fungi and lichens, invoking the sense of a landscape unchanged by the passage of millennia.

As we walk, we can hear nothing but the glen, so deep into the landscape it's like nothing else exists. Continuing along each side of the stream as little weathered wooden bridges carry us through the landscape, as readily as the water cascades through this glen, both in the stream and tumbling down the steep sides of the gorge in many spots. On we go, over bridges, up roughly hewn stone steps, and along slippery narrow ledges, every now and then finding a stone wall, or feature to remind us of the Victorian influence on the glen.

The route continues for several kilometres and is easily one of the prettiest and most magical places I have ever visited in my life. We are both thoroughly enchanted.

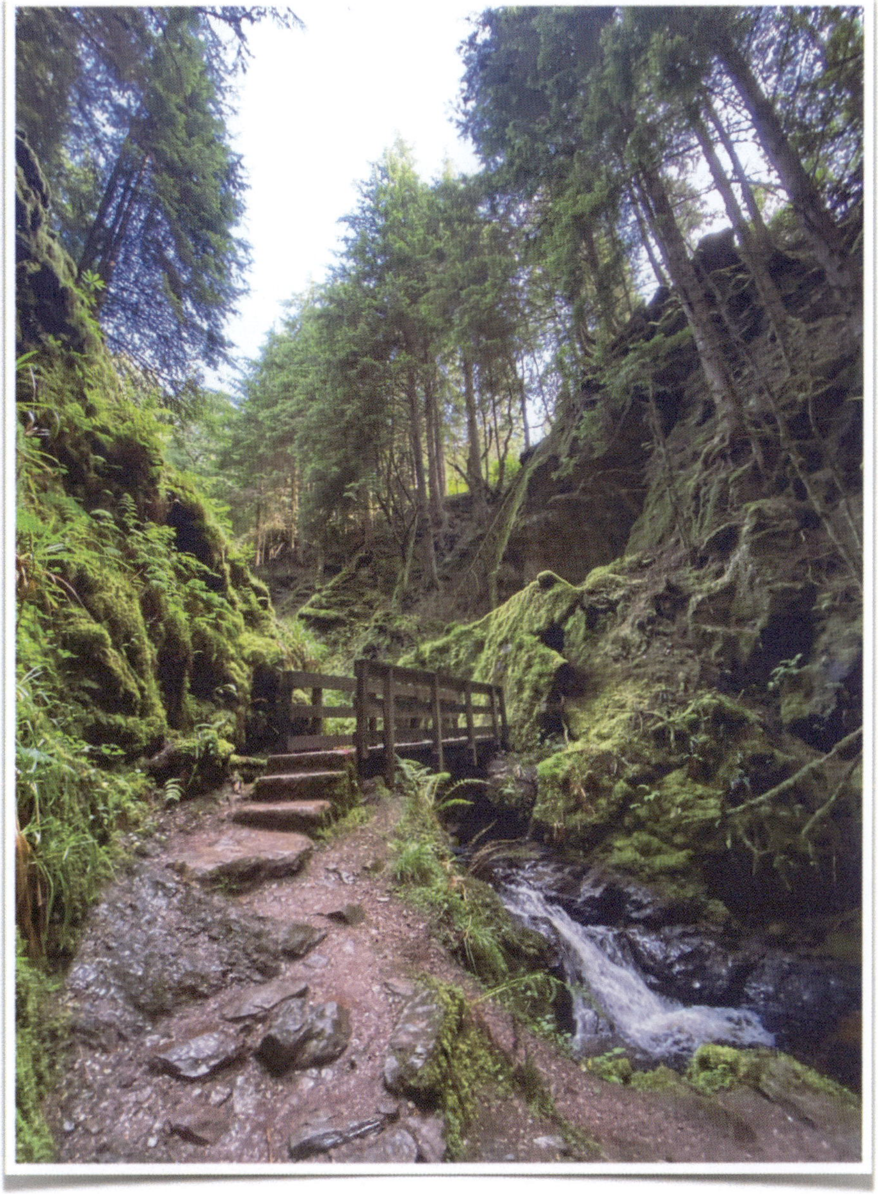

Another bridge and then steps, slopes and more roughly carved out path brings us daylight and a forestry path where we meet two ladies and stop for a chat. They started at Benmore Botanic Gardens and are heading for Puck's Glen, while we're heading on, linking up Puck's Glen with a forestry walk, and a walk called the Big Trees trail. We take the broad forest track up to the viewpoint.

As we round the next corner, enjoying the sunshine on our faces before we enter the dense forestry again for the Big Trees trail, we hear a familiar mewing as a buzzard comes into sight. We see plenty of buzzards and red kites back in South Wales, but always excited to see a bird of prey, we watch as it comes closer. Beside me, Stuart sets up the camera we borrowed from his dad, ready to capture him. He gets some shots, and we watch for a while before he soars up the steep escarpment, disappearing into the distance.

Our walk ends with the Big Trees Trail, and it lives up to its name. The information on this place says some of the trees here are more than a hundred years old, and I can believe it. Above us, soaring impossibly high until they disappear into the sky are Californian redwoods, Western hemlocks, and

Douglas firs, while beneath us lies a world of rocks and mosses, fungi in colours I have never seen before. Little red and white spotted fly agaric litter the forest floor, we feel like we've fallen into a fairytale, and teeny, tiny little white capped mushrooms grow between the wood sorrel and moss, making a magical, enchanting scene on the spongy and fuzzy forestry floor.

By the time we get back to the van, we have taken almost 400 pictures between us. This place has been an utter dream of magical prehistoric rainforest and lush, green loveliness.

What a day it's been! Tomorrow we're planning our first Munro and our second mountain as we plan to climb Ben Vorlich. The forecast is cold but dry so we head off towards the tonight's park up, right at the start of tomorrow's hike, Loch Earn just a few miles away.

The drives are as exciting as the walks and adventures. Around every corner there's another stunning view, another thing to feast your eyes on as Scotland delivers on every point.

It's getting late by the time we get to Loch Earn and there are a lot of people here. Several people are camping in tents at the shoreline, and they sit laughing around campfires while children play on hastily constructed rope swings. Vans line the Loch along the road, but we find a space and get settled for the night. I make hunter's chicken and by the time we've eaten and had a quick shower, we're both ready to fall into bed, another day well spent.

## Day 5: 24th September

By 9am we are up eating breakfast and discussing just how busy this spot is. It wasn't until this morning we realised it was Saturday, we've clearly gone full feral, I haven't even looked at a watch for days!

We already read that Ben Vorlich is a popular Munro because it's considered to be 'moderate' with no major scrambles. As I shovel granola into my mouth, I watch the procession of hikers with rucksacks and poles head off on a hike we'll be following them on very soon.

We've marked off two potential peaks in a single hike, Ben Vorlich and Stuc a Chroin, a challenging part circular coming in at around 14km. This will require peaking Ben Vorlich and then continuing on to an unseen, rockier more scrambly peak behind.

We often plan mega long routes, and then make decisions as we walk about whether we do the whole route or cut it down, so let's see where the day takes us and get started. It's forecast to feel like minus 3 at the peak so I wear several layers on top and a base layer under my hiking trousers.

We leave the van parked at the rough unofficial parking alongside the loch. By the time we leave, the whole strip is vans and cars parked up as hikers make the most of the sunny Saturday on this popular hill. Heading down the road, the right turn towards the farm is signposted and we follow the trail, through gates and over stiles, past a grand farmhouse covered in vibrant red Virginia Creeper up the walls. Slowly we start to climb alongside the forestry and glen of Ardvorlich, rising and exposing more and more beautiful views of the loch below.

It's a glorious day, we've been so lucky with the weather so far this trip and by the time we are at the top of the glen, I'm perching myself on a rock to peel off layers, including my base layer, which means stripping down to my knickers and putting my hiking trousers back on. As I try to do this as discretely as possible (and fail) Stuart giggles at my exposed underwear, teasingly pretending to take photographs as several people walk past watching us quizzically.

The well laid trail rises, over a bridge and past a hydro-electric dam, giving the first views of the peak. An easy-to-follow stone path takes us higher and higher as we start to gain some serious elevation, giving us near aerial views of the surrounding countryside, lochs, and mountains. It's a beautifully clear day, high white clouds scutter across the sky and it feels like summer, despite being the end of September. It makes for warm walking!

The mountain itself is bare, no trees, just grasses and bracken surround us as we follow the path, cross tiny streams, and head up towards the peak. We come to a flattish plateau, leading the path on towards the steepest part yet. Here we decide we're not taking another step until we've eaten something, so we find a couple of rocks and sit down for a well-earned rest, a drink, and some sustenance.

After a little while, we're off again, up the path on the steepest part of the hike so far. The peak above us, and the steep drop off to our left makes for a dramatic scene as the long ridge curves around and the escarpment falls away dramatically. I assume at this stage I look like I'm dying because hikers descending start to pass on words of encouragement about how we are almost there as they pass us.

And we are! A few more steps and the trig is visible, right on the edge of the ridge. There are a few people reaching the trig with us, so we stop and chat, take some photos for people and have some taken ourselves, someone offers me their hip flask and I oblige, enjoying my first swig of Scottish single malt on Scottish soil.

Then we stand and enjoy the view for a while. As we've now come to expect, there are nothing but mountains in every direction, rolling peaks and lochs as far as the eye can see, as the sunny, bright day leaves the view clear across Scotland.

The top of Ben Vorlich is flat and long with another cairn a little way away on the furthest end. I can also now see Stuc a Chroin looking less than inviting beyond a considerable descent and then an ascent over a boulder field. I ask Stuart how he feels about doing the longer route we originally marked out, and he replies, "I will walk there", pointing to the cairn on the furthest end of the peak, "I am not going there", pointing to Stuc a Chroin. I'm inclined to think he has a point if we want to be able to use our legs tomorrow. We are supposed to be on holiday after all!

It's cold but clear at the peak, warmer than the minus 3 windchill that was forecast but cool enough to justify pulling some layers back on. On this sunny Saturday, the flat top of Ben Vorlich is teaming with people, chatting, sitting, walking.

If you ever want to know why people climb mountains, even though it's hard, climb to the top of a busy one and judge the mood, you'll soon have your answer. Everyone we meet is bright, chatty, and jovial as we walk along to the cairn and find a spot to sit and have lunch.

There's a commotion at the end as people are discussing whether there are deer in the valley below. We've been able to hear the stags bellowing across the countryside as we've travelled, but we haven't set eyes on a red deer yet. A couple of men are saying they can see maybe as many as 60 or 80 deer in the valley below and I suddenly remember I've been carrying a pair of binoculars in my rucksack for about the last 2 years and haven't taken them out once. I dig them out and although they are hard to see even through the binoculars, there are a large herd of deer beneath us in the valley, and a smaller group of stags on a peat shelf a little way away.

It's such a still, calm day, Stuart gets some amazing drone shots from the top, showing a unique perspective of the entire peak that is hard to get when you're standing on it. We hang around for ages, enjoying the views, before deciding to descend from the back and then join the path we'd have taken if we'd climb Stuc a Chroin.

This turns out to be a mistake, and it turns a lovely day out into a muddy, boggy, difficult descent, navigating peat bogs, flow water, and tiny streams. By the time we rejoin the path we ascended on, we're tired after a long descent. There's a lot to be said for paths!

We bump into a couple who did go on and do Stuc a Chroin and after hearing them regale the boulder fields and scree descent, we're glad we opted to stick to just one peak.

We get back to the van tired but happy after a thoroughly enjoyable hike. It's already quite late so we decide to eat here and stay a second night at this spot. Stuart cooks an easy meal, and we fall asleep in front of the television.

# Day 6: 25th September

We were so tired last night we didn't make any plans, so this morning we need to decide what's next. We need some shopping and fuel, so after consulting Google maps to see what we have pinned, we decide on a supermarket run in Perth and then onto The Hermitage, a glen walk we've marked off, east of here.

I've also been doing some reading this morning on Scotland's Golden Eagle population and the Cairngorms is marked off as a good place for possible sightings on the mainland. We make a vague plan to head there next, I just need to decide which hill we'll attempt there.

So that's it, we're finished with Loch Lomond and the Trossachs National Park for now. It's been the loveliest few days and it's hard to believe we have barely got started yet, less than a week in and this is shaping up to be the trip of a lifetime.

We pull out from our park up at Loch Earn and follow the road alongside the loch, but the Trossachs has not stopped giving, a red squirrel leaps out onto the road in front of us! Stuart stops the van, and we watch him for a while, scrambling down the road a little way before he finally gets to the other side, running up a tree to the right of us. What a way to start the day!

Next, it's time for a not-so-exciting trip to Tesco in Perth. Shopping isn't my favourite thing to do but travelling in a van does mean the essentials have to be catered for and the fridge is starting to look a bit bare. It's time to restock.

The Tesco run ends up being more exciting than anticipated as we realise how much Scottish fare they offer, and how different the store is to the Tesco stores at home. We must look like such tourists squealing at haggis, square sausages, venison, and something called beef olives. We settle on some square sausages, some highland venison meatballs, and the beef olives, I grab a bottle of Scottish single malt they have on offer, then we fill the rest of the trolley and head off to pay. Stuart tops up the diesel on the way out and we make our way to The Hermitage, a walk in Perthshire a few miles away.

This stretch of magical Perthshire forest along the River Braan was originally used as a pleasure ground for aristocrats, specifically the Dukes of Atholl and it started to take shape in the early 1700s. We're hoping that in addition to the historic landscape and stunning nature trail, we might see the resident beavers along the river and tick another thing off our wish list. There's also an exciting cave feature on the trail, and something called Ossian's Hall of Mirrors.

We come in past Inver Holiday Park and stop at the first small car park that gives access to the trail. I'm hungry so we have brie and bacon wraps before we head off. We travel light today, no big rucksacks. Although we don't realise it yet, the trail will end up being more than 8km long by the time we've ventured off it a few times to explore.

We walk from the car park up onto the old Military Road. Eventually road gives way to the Tay Forest, and we are treated to a broad pathed forestry walk lined with Douglas Firs soaring to the sky.

I stop to take pictures here, mostly of fungi, and capture boletes, blackening polypore, trooping funnel, birch polypore, russula, what seems like a hundred fly agaric, and many more mushrooms I couldn't dream to name. We're keen to get to the river part of the walk so we press on, and while I don't know it yet, I will spend the next three weeks regretting not foraging more in this area. I was so overwhelmed by how many varieties there were I didn't even pick dinner.

I'm only in my second-year learning about edible mushrooms, but I suspect if today is anything to go by, Scotland will be a lesson in the sheer number of fungi species available!

As we drop down out of the forestry, a thundering sound alerts us to the river. The trail goes to the right, but to the left we can see a waterfall down a narrower path that is not an official trail but has clearly been walked by many people.

Heading off-piste a little we make our way to the water, a wide, shallow river, wending its way through huge boulders and down ravines, creating deep endless pools, and roaring as it goes. The next bit requires leaping a few large rocks for a good view upstream towards a beautiful waterfall before us.

My mind is blown by the sheer beauty here. If I wrote this travelogue via my internal dialogue – and external one as we travelled – it would be lots of pages of "Ohhhh" and "Ahhhh" and "Oh my God, look at that!". Words really do not do justice to this place, and every time I feel like we've seen the most beautiful place in Scotland, something else comes along to send me into another frenzy of "Ohhhs" and "Ahhhhs".

Across the rocks we leap and in one of the pools created by the pattern of the river is the best part of a fallen Douglas fir. About halfway along it, it looks like some great creature has taken a giant bite. Upon closer inspection it's clear to see that it's lots of small bites, and while we don't see a beaver today, this fallen pine can stand as evidence that they are here!

Stuart gets the drone out, intending on flying it upstream towards the waterfall, so I tell him I'll head back to the path with the dog and start hopping boulders back onto solid ground. Here, I realise there's a tiny track along to the waterfall we're looking at, unable to shout my intentions back to Stuart over the roar of the water, I just head up that way anyway… He'll soon work it out.

I get right above the dramatic fall and start stepping out across the boulders that make up this stunning river landscape. I want to get out as far as I can and moving from boulder to boulder is a challenge, requiring me to shuffle on my bum and lowering myself down in some places. Nala has no such trouble and hops gracefully from rock to rock like the mountain goat she emulates.

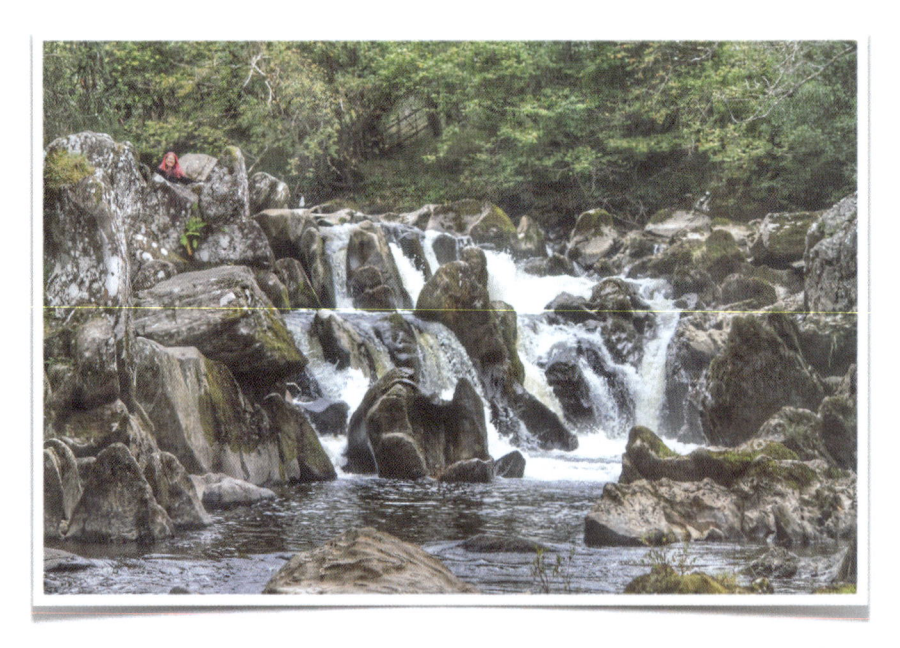

Eventually I get to the biggest boulder where the river narrows for a dramatic part of the fall, and it's so powerful and fast flowing that even from standing height the spray from the falls is covering me in a damp mist.

I can see Stuart slightly downstream with the drone controls in hand, but I can't catch sight of the drone. I'm not sure he can even see me, and I can't shout over the sound of the water to get his attention. After a few minutes I see the drone in the air, but even now I have no idea if he knows I'm here, I give a little wave, see him fly the drone back and make my way back to the riverbank where I've seen a possible narrow path to the lower section of the falls beneath me.

Back at the riverbank, I start to climb lower to access the bottom part of the fall. As I drop down to the riverbed, I fail to notice a branch above my head and hit it so hard, I'll have a small bruise and a graze for the next few days. I'm clambering out onto the lower part of the waterfall as Stuart appears. Being out on the fall, on the boulders that force the water through these narrow gaps is thrilling, the mist and spray hitting your face, and a deafening thunder of crashing water in your ears.

It's time to get back to the trail or this walk will never be over, though it's so beautiful, I could happily stay here forever! After hopping, stepping and shuffling back across the rocks, it's back up the bank, I'm still rubbing my head, surprised at how hard I've hit it when Stuart spots a tiny frog running up the mossy bank, so we stop to take some pictures.

We re-join the trail and I check the map to see that the next section includes a feature called Rumbling Bridge so off we go. The huge trees give the forest a cathedralesque feel, towering over us as we walk. There's the sense you've never walked among trees quite so tall, and it's not far from true. One of the tallest trees in the UK resides here, a Douglas Pine last measured at 201 feet.

When we finally get to the bridge, we discover is aptly named. The sheer spate of water pushing down this gorge is deafening and it feels as though the bridge is rumbling underneath us. I stay up on the bridge this time as Stuart clambers down the rocks for a closer look at this torrent of water, crashing through the boulders, narrowing into the tiniest space around a corner, and gushing under the bridge.

The next section of the walk takes us through more woodland, more fungi, and more towering firs!

To our right is the river, to our left we see the cave that gives The Hermitage its name. It's an odd, octagonal building that uses the rocks around it as part of the structure, giving it a cave-like feel.

The Hermitage is above the waterfall at Acharn, and the story goes that it was built by a hermit who stayed in this area, building the Hermitage and living in solitude here. It's a great story, but it is just that, as in reality it's a folly and part of the landscaping of the area, done in the 1700s for the Dukes of Atholl, as mentioned earlier. The place is full of these dramatic viewpoints, slightly tweaking the natural landscape to the full advantage of the viewer.

As we round the next corner, the noise tells us we've reached another dramatic fall and sure enough Black Linn Falls crashes down to our right. As we clamber down to the riverbank for a closer look, a tiny circular building appears above us, giving way to a picturesque stone bridge to the right of it.

This is Ossian's Hall, built in 1757 as the focal point of this extensive landscape. It's from the balcony of here you get the very best views of Black Linn falls, and so we walk up for a look.

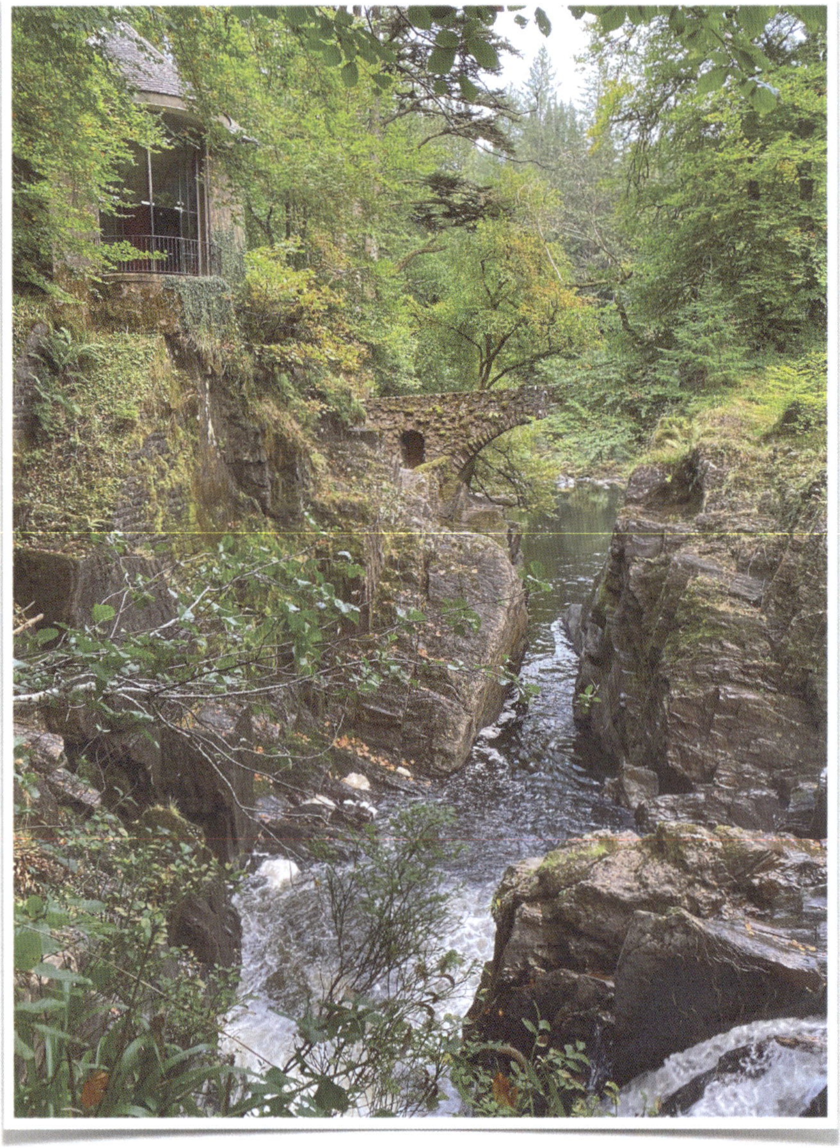

The views from here are out of this world and we stand for a while watching the forked falls, crash, and foam beneath us.

After a look at the tiny stone bridge, we're at the end of the features and viewpoints of this walk and it's time to head back to the van.

There's a small no overnighting sign in the car park, but it's out of season and there's already a VW T25 with its pop-top up, emitting dinner smells so we decide to risk it and tuck into a quiet corner for the evening. We often litter pick car parks as a form of payment on our travels, but it's spotless here.

It's already late so after dinner and a shower we sit and decide where next. We've already made the plan to head towards the Cairngorms to bag a Munro with the hope of seeing golden eagles.

After our research about sightings, we decide to hike up A'Chailleach. In the morning we'll head for the village of Newtonmore where we'll take the mountain track up to the start of the walk.

It's been another busy day and we're ready to fall into bed.

## Day 7: 26th September

I have one of those moments when I wake up where I have no idea at all where I am. That's the problem with waking up in the same bed in a different place every day, sometimes it takes a minute for the brain to catch up. It's almost 10am so we've slept in. As I pull the blinds back, I see the VW is still parked a little way away, windows all misted up. We're still the only two vans in the car park.

It's a big day today eagle hunting and Munro-bagging so we get a move on and hit the road. We head up the A9 to Newtonmore and I work as we drive. It's hard to focus on the laptop because the mountains here are beautiful!

The weather is changeable and we drive through sunshine and showers until we reach the village of Newtonmore. We take a left, along a road called Glen Road. It starts off lined with houses and is a well paved road, but slowly it gives way to open land and becomes a little bumpy trail, climbing higher and higher into the hills to our planned park up for the night, and the start of the hike.

There are several park ups along this road that would be perfect for campers. We don't see a soul! We carry on along the road, planning to be as close as possible to the start of the hike.

The hike is described as an easy 4km walk to the peak at 997 metres, and then the descent is back along the same route. What could possibly go wrong?

As we set off up the path, the sun beats down on us as we go through the deer gate and along what is a wide, mostly flat, well laid trail. The views are extraordinary. There's a river to our left, hills all around us, and as we walk, we try and work out from the map whether we can see the peak of A'Chailleach yet.

I check the map a little way along and realise we have just missed a left turn, we retrace back a few yards and see a tiny marker, just five small stones in a pile, but someone has laid out some smaller pebbles into the shape of an arrow, indicating the left turn we need (thank you, whoever you are, this turn is easily missed).

We clamber through the bracken on the narrow track and come to a wooden bridge crossing the stream at the point of a substantial waterfall. Over we go, and as we head along the river through bracken, heather, bog myrtle and other fauna, the trail becomes a lot less obvious. We're missing the solid stone path as we head along as it's very boggy at the riverbank, making every step a challenge. We cut left a little, rising above the bank in the hope we might find more solid ground, my feet sinking almost to the ankle with every step.

Every few hundred yards the dog disturbs a ptarmigan, and it flutters, panicked into the air. Onwards we walk, refusing to acknowledge the hard to navigate landscape, and not giving voice to the changing weather now spitting against the side of our faces. The path has gone, somewhere to the right in the bog.

Eventually we come to a stream, and it takes some navigating. This is the problem with going off-piste, but the terrain is impossible here. I can feel the water starting to penetrate my leather waterproof boots in places, and the driving rain that is falling intermittently has now breached the cuffs of my coat. We keep an eye on the sky but there's no sign of eagles so far, there's no sign of anything but rain.

As we climb the bank in front of us, we can now see the peak of A'Chailleach in the clouds. To our left we can see a small tin hut and caught in another shower of rain we head for it.

Our first Scottish bothy, and we're grateful for it. The weather has taken a considerable turn for the worst and combined with the already boggy ground it's not making for fun walking. The bothy is cute as anything! The outside is corrugated tin so we're not expecting much but when we get inside its timber lined and offers a fair amount of protection from the 'elements', which are currently pounding on the roof quite noisily! There's a tiny table with a notebook left open and although we don't have a pen, we do thumb through and read some of the comments, including many about seeing golden eagles in the glen. The walls are covered in graffiti, chalked, scratched, gouged, and pencilled with names dating back to the 1920s and we stay a while reading the messages and dates until the inclement weather passes.

A little while later and we're off again, making some serious ascent now as we climb towards A'Chailleach. I have walked some mountains, and many without suitable trails, but I don't think I have ever been anywhere so wet and boggy as this. I am drenched, the peat so deep in places that only my poles are keeping me upright, but we push on. As we start the final kilometre, the wind changes direction and the rain picks up again.
By now it's cold, we're at mountain elevation and what was rain a little way down the hill, is now sharp, icy sleet and snow driving into our faces as the gusts take a more serious turn. Nala is crouched behind Stuart's legs, cowering from the wind and icy shards, and it doesn't take much more than a few metres before we both stop, look at each other and start laughing. We both agree to

call it a day, and it really sucks because in all my years of hiking, I have never failed to complete a peak. It's horrid here, visibility is at about five metres, and the sharp snow hitting my face is just the cherry on the top of already unpleasant hiking conditions. We turn heel, Nala looking relieved and start to descent.

By the time we get back to the bothy, the sun is out and warm on our faces. Isn't that just typical? We briefly consider climbing again, but the swirling clouds around the peak, and keen wind give us other ideas. Besides, we were up here for golden eagles, and it's evident they have the good sense to be elsewhere on this awful day.

Descending, we cut down to the original path we should have taken on the way up. Yes, it's boggy but no worse than the way we ascended and it's pretty walking here alongside the river. I am drenched, and every time the day dries me out, another rain shower moves in and soaks me again. My feet are wet as the bog has soaked through the leather entirely. My waterproof boots are waterproof no more and will now need drying and waxing before the next walk. It's a quiet walk, neither of us with much to say.

We get back to the bridge, cross it and I pick up a large stone, adding it to the tiny cairn we nearly lost our way at, to help the next hikers who come through here see the turn. Eventually, we trundle back to the van. We have been joined by another van with Dutch plates while we've been hiking.

By now there's howling wind and sideways rain, and whoever is in that van clearly has more sense than us, as we don't see them outside at all.

I'm really, really disappointed at not completing the walk as we get back to the van (although reliving the day through writing this has reminded me exactly why we turned back).

Stuart offers to cook to cheer me up, and we have the beef olives we picked up at the supermarket. I feel like these things are Scotland's best kept secret and I'm determined to attempt to make my own at home. They contain no olives, and are made of paper-thin slices of steak, wrapped around sausage meat. Dinner is delicious but the evening is a little subdued, both of us feeling the defeat of the day. No eagles, no Munro bagged! I sit and work a while and we spend the evening lounging around chatting and watching television while the rain and winds howl outside.

## Day 8: 27th September

The weather hasn't improved since last night, and this morning we decide to meander towards the east coast where the forecast is brighter. My parents went to a place called Rosemarkie near Inverness last time they were here and saw dolphins so that's the direction we're heading but it's quite a long way away. We check the map to find somewhere en-route and add Loch Ness to the itinerary. You can't come to Scotland and miss out Loch Ness!

A friend has messaged me and recommended a nearby place called Ruthven Barracks, so we add that to the route for the day, add in another waterfall near Loch Ness, and plan to end the day at the loch side.

The barracks are just a couple of miles away so before long we're pulling into the small parking area alongside them. The large ruinous buildings stand impressively on a small mound, giving it the feel of a castle.

Ruthven Barracks was built by George II's government after the failed Jacobite uprising of 1715. In 1745, the barracks were attacked by more than 300 Jacobites but they failed to take the building. A year later they came back, more heavily armed and forced the barracks' surrender. The historic building is now in the hands of Historic Scotland and is open to the public for free.

There's not enough to do here to justify a whole day out, but it was well worth a visit. We spend an hour walking around the rooms and stables of the barracks, reading the Historic Scotland information and taking in the feel of this well-preserved historic building. There's a stunning rainbow behind the barracks – we've seen at least one every day since the first one on The Cobbler walk – so we spend a while enjoying its colours, and enjoying the views of the Cairngorms in the distance. In comes the rain again, signalling our time to leave and head east towards Loch Ness.

The next drive is of 50 miles or so of scenic road. I try and work on my laptop as we travel but don't get very far as the winding, narrow roads make me feel a little nauseous. Thankfully the views are to die for, I make do with relaxing and enjoying the lush greenery of the landscape as we leave the Cairngorms and make our way east towards the coast.

Loch Ness is vast! I've read many times that it is 23 miles long, but you really cannot appreciate how big it is until you drive alongside it. As we get to the area, it's hotel after hotel, inns and restaurants, and more hotels to boot. I feel like we've driven into the most popular area of Scotland so far.

We've come a few miles along the loch before stopping for our next destination, another small walk to a feature called the Falls of Foyer, a waterfall that is one of the loch's tributaries. There's a small free car park with toilets, and a little shop and café. The car parking is up a steep slope and there's a sign warning long vehicles not to enter. I get out to watch Stuart in, and we manage it fine in our 7.5m Sprinter. The falls trail is across the road and isn't a long walk, so we pull on coats and get started.

It's a short, steep walk down to the Falls viewpoint. We clamber down the steps and enter the small fenced off area. The waterfall is a long drop fall, about 50 metres, and while many of the photos we saw showed a broad, long cascade of water levels are low today and it's not as impressive as it must be at other times.

The pool the falls are plunging into is huge, deep, and wide, before it narrows back into the river and eventually joins Loch Ness. We continue walking and drop down a further level for another view of the falls. This turns out to offer a better vantage point and we stand watching for a while before strolling through the forestry.

The walk takes us through a pine forest, where we see more red squirrels, but no pine martens, despite them being reported in this area. The sun is out and glitters through the trees, dappling Autumn light all around us, and lighting up the orange floor of the forest, which is awash with pine needles and not much else. Here we see the first signs of Autumn, where in the gorge beneath us the different trees are starting to change into a kaleidoscope of reds, yellows, and oranges.

It's a short walk, so before long we're climbing back up to the road and back to the car park above us. Stuart pops into the shop for some milk and a couple of other bits, and we look at the map for a pull-in alongside Loch Ness we might be able to spend the night, and head off.

As forecast, driving east did drive us out of the bad weather we had in the Cairngorms. I don't feel as though we made the most of that area, but hopefully this won't be our only trip to Scotland. Loch Ness is still and the water sparkles in the sunshine. We don't see any sign of Nessie but there are a few pleasure boats out on the water. We find the lay-by park up we'd chosen alongside the loch by a small picnic area and pull in.

I hop out, excited to get to the water's edge and as I run down the slope, promptly slip on the wet grass, fall, and slide the rest of the way down the grass verge on my bottom. Stuart is easily amused, laughing from the van where I leave him to go and explore. As I cut through the hedges to the side of the loch I can hear screaming and laughing. When I reach the pebbled shore, I can see why. A few feet left of me are some youngsters skinny dipping. I avert my eyes and walk the other way, but the girls have seen me, and they are clamouring to get out of the water and cover up.

Loch Ness is a beautiful place, the sheer size of it overwhelming. After a short walk along the waterfront, I come back to the van and as the sun sets over Loch Ness, we settle down for the evening. I cook the Highland venison meatballs we bought, with some pasta and homemade sauce, and then we sit for a while discussing our plans.

Just before we left home a solar storm was predicted for the end of the month and this means there's a good chance of seeing the northern lights. The plan is to get to the North Coast for this so for the first time we need some fixed, time specific plans.

We can see Urquhart Castle on the other shore, but the loch is so long it's almost 50 miles away. That one will have to keep for another visit, and we decide to head straight to Rosemarkie tomorrow, and then north in time for the last couple of days of the month and hopefully the solar storm and the Aurora.

Scotland is exhausting! We fall into bed after another long day and we're soon asleep.

## Day 9: 28th September

We're planning our North Coast adventure around the Aurora now, so we've scheduled to push on a fair bit today. First stop, Rosemarkie, just north of Inverness. From there we'll head North to Brora Beach where we're planning an overnight stop.

Before we get started, we need some clean washing. Road trip excitement galore! We check online and find a Revolution Laundry at the Esso fuel station at the Muir of Ord with room across the road to park up for a while. Stuart takes the washing and organises the laundry while I sit in the back of the van and work for an hour. Once that's done, we fill up at the fuel station, ask permission to refill our water at their tap, refill, and head off for some fun.

As we drive towards the coast, my mind wanders to fish and chips. You can't beat fish and chips by the sea. It's a pretty drive to Rosemarkie, where we join the well-known NC500 route for the first time. It's a tiny place. We head down the hill, straight for Chanonry Point car park, right on the seafront. It's marked as not suitable for motorhomes. We're technically a van and not that wide so we pull in and we do manage to fit in a single space, thankfully.

It won't be a long hike today, just a walk along the beach. Stuart packs the cameras and we head out. The headland is very small so we're virtually on the beach. Chanonry Point lighthouse stands to our left, bright and white, with yellow trim. A short, stumpy lighthouse compared to many around the UK. By the end of the trip we'll realise that every lighthouse in Scotland is built on a very similar design and they're all styled the same way.

We could see seals from the van driving in to the car park and almost as soon as we get onto the beach we can see more seals in the water. Within just a few minutes we see a dolphin breach the surface across the water in Avoch Bay, then two, three, four, chasing each other through the waves. What a display! We stand for a while watching and taking bad photos of the dolphins play, the seals bobbing around the bay, and the seabirds sitting on the waves.

After a while we walk the length of the beach up towards the lighthouse and make our way around the point to explore. Across the water is Fort George, an imposing military fort on the sea. We carry on around the head, walking up the sandy beach, throwing stones for Nala and scanning the the sea for more seals and dolphins. It's a lovely walk, on what is a blustery but dry day. It's great to be at the coast! We don't see any more dolphins, but we do see a few more grey seals as we make our way back to the van and on to the next location!

Brora is about 45 miles away, and we plan to pick up fish and chips on the way. It's time to move on. As Stuart drives up the coast, I search online for some nearby fish and chip shops and find we find a takeaway and restaurant called the Bear's Den in Brora. It has decent reviews and so we park up in Brora and I leave Stuart in the van while I go and get our dinner. The takeaway is attached to the restaurant so it's not like a traditional fish and chip shop, and the meals are cooked fresh, which I'm more than happy with. Once our food is cooked we make our way down to Brora Beach where we plan to spend the night.

As we drive down onto Brora seafront, we see parking on our left alongside the estuary. That could make a nice overnight park up, but we'll check the sea front first. Here we find a small, circular car park and we pull in, facing the sea. First things first, dinner. Rather than hop in the back, we stay in the cab watching the sea as we eat delicious fish and chips.

Once we've eaten and refuelled, we get out and look at our surroundings. There aren't any no camping signs to deter us and it's a lovely, picturesque spot. We've been so lucky with the weather, but for the first time since we drove over the border, I am cold! I pop on a scarf and hat, and we clamber down onto the beach for a walk.

It's a tiny little seafront community. Just a few beach hut style houses and a couple of cottages, an estuary to our left and a long, sandy bay with rocky sections and plenty of boulders. The waves coming into the estuary are huge! To the other side of us is a large area on the seafront with 12-foot chain link fence around it, it looks out of place. After a closer look we realise it's the local campsite.

We take a breezy walk up the beach with Nala, throwing stones, clambering out onto rocky outcrops, looking in rock pools and exploring the surroundings before finally calling an end to our long day and climbing back up to the car park.

It's almost sunset and as Nala insists on meeting one of the neighbourhood dogs, we get chatting to its owner, who assures us we'll be fine to stay overnight on the seafront. We're the only ones here as we settle down for the evening. One last check of the long-range aurora forecasts, which still look good for the end of the month, and we are off to bed with the aim of continuing north tomorrow.

## Day 10: 29th September

It's a stunningly beautiful day in Brora, and I awake to the sound of the waves of the high tide. With the beach just three metres from the van, and the tide up high onto the rocks, it's loud. Stuart gets up, makes me a coffee, and takes Nala outside. I lie in bed, watching the ocean from the side window. The sun is high in the sky, but it's a windy morning and the waves crashing into the estuary are sizeable.

I have a considerable lie in, watching the view from the window, drinking coffee, watching heron on the beach, two or three of them, and myriad other seabirds too. Stuart has the camera out and is taking pictures, while I'm just storing memories and taking it easy.

Mid-morning, I drag myself up, get dressed and we walk up the beach a little way. We watch a surfer across the estuary getting thrown about like a ragdoll in the surf as seabirds sit on the waves, both making the most of the rough seas. Brora is a beautiful place, and our first coastal stop off has been a delight. It's time to move on though, so we get organised and get back on the road.

Traditionally, people follow the coast road north from here, all part of the NC500 route but we're making it up as we go and we've decided to leave the coast and the NC500 again and take a logging road up to the North Coast and visit Flow Country, an area of Scotland marked by peatland and wetland.

We're heading for the Forsinard Flows National Nature reserve, but we're in no rush to get there. The road is quiet, just us and the odd logging truck to pull in for. We pull over and swap seats and I drive for a while as Stuart flies the drone behind the van, filming us and the scenery as we travel. Then as Stuart takes over the wheel again, I sit and hang out of the open window, filming myself and the miles of countryside around me as we go. Just a bit of silly fun en-route!

This is the flattest landscape we've seen to date, and all around us are rivers, waterfalls, rolling hills and streaks of wetlands across the landscape. It's beautiful here and as Autumn deepens the hills are starting to turn a deep orange.

Soon we're at the nature reserve and we see the wetland viewpoint tower to the left. We pull over and get our walking boots on, and amble over to the viewpoint on very boggy ground. We've walked the wrong way, the visitors centre, and the path from it to our right.

When we get to the tower, it's all little stone paths around bogs and marshes. The weather is murky, and clouds are blowing through exposing the hills in the distance and then hiding them again. We're standing at the bottom of the tower taking it all in when

Nala goes to take a drink from a shallow looking pool. Suddenly, she's in up to her neck and is scrambling to get out of the water, peat sliding off her, muddy, and indignant. For a while there's nothing Stuart and I can do but laugh. Nala is less amused. She's going to need a shower before we get back in the van.

We explore the tower and the flows around, wandering around the pathways, reading the little engraved markers and nature information along the way.

It's a short walk around the designated boardwalk, but it's very picturesque and interesting, despite the grey day. There's another group of local people here, and we stop and chat for a little while as they tell us what a treat we're in for with the West Coast to look forward to.

It's been amazing so far, Scotland is magical.

We have a slightly bigger hike planned just a mile down the road, so we make our way back to the van where we give Nala a full wash, with shampoo, with our outdoor shower before we move on.

About a mile down the road, we pull up on the left at a logging place where there are signs for The Forsinain Trail. The signs say the walk is a circular walk of about 5km.

As I'm reading the noticeboard, full of information about Flow Country and about how the peat bogs here are as deep as two double decker buses, Stuart chats with a local trucker working the logging route. When we're at home he's an HGV driver, and he's clearly enjoying a busman's holiday imagining work in another scenario.

A quick lunch and we pull on our walking boots as the sun comes out.

The trail is beautiful. We walk along a wide logging track with the river to our right, meandering around wetlands and scanning the countryside for some wildlife.

The route takes us past a couple of rural dwellings and then across open country and It's not long before we are rewarded as we see a hind and her baby that have been separated by a deer fence. We stand for a while and watch them walk the boundary, trying to find a way to get back to each other.

We can hear stag bellowing and we are soon treated to some spectacular views. On the other side of the river are two herds of deer, both with thirty or forty hinds and near those, stags roam across the wetlands, the dense forestry acting as a backdrop.

We stop for a moment and just observe, taking photographs and sharing our delight at seeing so many deer so close.

Eventually the road and trail end, and we can't see where we're supposed to go next. On the sign back at the van, it showed a circular route which means we should be going to the right. I regret not taking a picture of it, but there's no route to follow from this point so we head out across open country, cutting right where we hope we'll join up with the remainder of the circular walk.

There's a hill ahead of us and suddenly forty or fifty deer appear at the top of it, clear as anything against the now blue sky. I get the binoculars out and for a while we're frozen to the spot watching the display. Standing very still, we whisper to each other, and snap photographs.

We get going again, but we really have no idea which way. The trail route on the sign showed a route through forestry so we continue to cut right, eyeing up the forestry on the other side of the river. It's boggy and getting boggier by the minute, this is Flow Country after all.

By the time we get to the river, it's clear it's too fierce and deep to cross. We're forced to abandon all hope at getting to the forestry and we follow the river back towards the road, watching the deer in the long grasses on the other side of the river as we go. In the very boggy areas, all I can think about is the sign that says there are peat bogs here deeper than two double decker buses and, on several occasions, I have slight wobbly moments about it swallowing me up, a cause of great amusement to Stuart.

After a couple of kilometres squelching through peat bogs and laughing and joking about the Scottish tourism board putting up signs when they have apparently only built half the walk, we see the road ahead. It's still at least another kilometre away but it looks like we can join where we started, and we'll be on solid ground again.

That's not all we see, as to our left two stags square up on an area of grassland, bellowing at each other, facing off to rut. This is one of the sights we came to Scotland for so we watch a while as they walk around each other, heads down, ready to lock antlers. The moment never comes and the stag on the right, who is visibly smaller, turns heel and springs away into the distance. This action disturbs a group of hinds who churn across the wetlands before us, throwing up sprays of water and tiny rainbows at their feet. A magical cavalry of beauty, splashing through the countryside.

We get to a couple of streams, one after the other. Both require balancing on wire fences to get over and back to the track. With lots of giggles and a few heart-stopping moments, we're both across and back on the road. Half a kilometre along the trail we started on and we're back to the van.

I look at the sign as we get back and I can honestly say I have no idea if we missed a turning, or whether the trail hadn't been completed. Still, it all makes for a great adventure.

Both spots we stopped at along the logging road (A897) would have made for a scenic overnight park up, at the Forsinard Flows tower and the Forsinain Trail, but we are pushing on to the North Coast, the clock ticking down to the predicted solar storm. By now we're tired, our third walk of the day complete. It's about twenty miles to our park up at Sandside Bay Beach so we're back on the road.

It's late and by the time we get to Sandside Bay, there's not much to see. There's a no overnighting sign on the road on the way in, but we're alone and without a soul for miles we decide to risk it and park up alongside the beach next to the toilet block. We're both exhausted. I sit and catch up with some work as Stuart cooks us square sausage, we're still trying out local fare!

After a quick shower, we fall asleep in front of the TV.

## Day 11: 30th September

I've been making vague noises about going wild swimming once we hit the coast, but as we wake up the van is rocking with wind, and rain is hammering down on the roof. I somehow don't think today will be the day.

Stuart is the first to brave the outside as he goes to use the toilet block. When he comes back, he shows me a sign he's taken a picture of warning that the beach is radioactive! Well, that's a first for us. It's not too much to worry about for a day visitor, and we can see levels of radiation are very low on the beach but stronger across the bay on the rocky shore of the disused nuclear power station that is causing the radioactive pollution. No matter what, I don't think this will be my first wild swimming location, although growing webbed feet might be handy for travelling Scotland.

The rain eases off and we decide to brave the weather and take a walk. Radiation aside, Sandside Bay is a stunning stretch of golden yellow sands. We walk the length of the beach and back with the dog. The recent bad weather has churned up huge swathes of seaweed and dumped them on the beach and as we walk, we marvel at the vibrant greens, yellows, and bright pinks in the weed, an array of colours across the landscape.

Towards the far end of the beach freshwater runs down a valley, onto the beach and into the sea. This water is brown, peat shelves washed downstream after a long dry summer, and as it joins the crystal blue waters it refuses to mix, creating a stream of rust brown water right out into the bay.

We time the walk back to the van very badly, and get caught in what can only be described as a dumping of water from the sky, soaking us through within a few seconds. Stuart runs ahead with Nala, laughing and shouting as Nala leaps around him wondering what all the excitement is about. When I get up off the beach, he and her are sheltered in a small area behind the toilet block.

We're both hungry so it's time to sit, have some lunch and work out what's next.

Although we skipped most of the East Coast, we do want to say we've done the most Northerly points and tick off some touristy places. We plan a route that takes us east and back, incorporating Duncansby Stacks, Dunnet Head, and John o' Groats, tagging a sandy, north facing bay to end the day to coincide with the forecast for the solar flare starting this evening. It's almost sixty miles to the next location, and we have several stops marked off, which means it's time to get back on the road.

The drive is beautiful, but I try and use the downtime wisely and work on the road to the next location.

Our first stop today is John O'Groats, one end of the longest distance between two inhabited points on the British mainland, 876 miles from Land's End in Cornwall at the other end. We pull up into the car park and it's busy with tourists. There's a shop and facilities, a ferry port and the iconic white sign showing distances to Land's End and many famous cities. We grab a few pictures and hop back in the van; aware we have lots of locations and at least one hike to get covered today.

Next, it's the hike. We drive along a few miles of coast road, impeded by the sheep as we go and eventually end up parked up at Duncansby Stack lighthouse, another stumpy lighthouse, styled in white, yellow, and black. There are a few parking spaces here and we remark how this would be suitable for an overnight stop, though it may get a little windy out here on the headland. It's time to walk along the cliffs to the stacks, so we get out in the wind, grateful it's at least bright and clear.

The Duncansby Stacks are two pointy sea stacks out on some headland in the far Northeast of Scotland. From the car park it's about 6km round to walk and see them and back.

We set off and I'm immediately glad to have put my walking boots on, it's boggy along the cliffs but it's a beautiful walk. We soon come to the most Northerly trig point in the UK and grab a picture, then start walking along the cliffs to the stacks. I scan the sea to our left in the hope of seeing some great sea-mammal breach the waves, but I don't get lucky.

However, soon we get to a small, deep inlet and as we watch the waves crash into it creating a deafening roar, the stacks in the distance. Here we can see seals playing in the huge waves that are being created by the fissure in the rocks.

We follow the path round as it gets steeper and more slippery until finally the stacks are in sight. We're right on the very north coast of the UK and it feels like it too, as the dramatic cliff lined coastline roars beneath us, the azure sea catching the sun with every turn of the wave.

We stroll for a while looking for seals, or maybe bigger sea creatures in the waves until we get close to the stacks. This moody, tumultuous coastline is loud, vivid, and unforgettable. Heavy dark clouds start to roll in over the stacks, and we sneak over the fence to get closer to these craggy towers for a look.

You can continue along the headland here and get slightly closer to the stacks, another half a kilometre along the jagged cliffs but we decide that's far enough for today in the biting wind, and start the walk back towards the lighthouse to move onto the next location.

Our next stop today is Dunnet Head, the most northerly point of mainland Britain. The area is an RSPB reserve, and you can park right on the head so there's no big hike.

Again, we park up near the lighthouse and walk out onto the cliffs. This too would make a great overnight spot if you wanted to be up on the cliffs, but we have beach plans. There's a small walkway here to a viewpoint, ending in a fence. We climb the fence and walk along the cliff where waterfalls run down the grassy cliffs and drop hundreds of feet into the sea. We're soon joined by another daring couple, so we stop for a chat and take a few pictures for them, and them for us, before stopping a while on the clifftop and enjoying the view. I think this is one of the highest cliffs I have ever stood on and the view down the rough, jagged rocks beneath us to the ocean is vertigo-inducing.

This dramatic view is created by millions of years of sedimentary rock, giving way to the ocean in drops of hundreds of feet, interspersed with lush green ledges down to boulder beaches as land and sea fight to the finish, tide after tide.

Today has been a real treat and we get back to the van a little windswept but feeling fresh and invigorated. Last stop tonight is our overnight spot, and we arrive at Castletown Beach just before the sunset, pink and gold streaks creating a candyfloss sky as the tide comes in.

We park up for the evening, and stand in the van doorway, sheltered from the chill, snapping photos and taking in the view.

Despite the forecast for Aurora, the alert never comes, which is a shame as it's a clear evening. We're one of three vans here this evening, and so we relax and have some dinner and look for another north facing location for tomorrow night.

## Day 12: 1st October

Hello October!

You wouldn't think it was October to wake up here on this sunny day on the North Coast of Scotland. The temperature is incredibly mild, although it's very windy, and the white horses out there on the waves tell us it's a rough day at sea.

I think we must have died in the night because we've woken up with the sunrise and we're in heaven. What a beautiful white sandy beach.

By breakfast the tide is well and truly coming in, white-tipped turquoise waves roll in one after another, crashing on the shore as we sit and eat enjoying the scenes.

I make a decision, pulling on my swimming shorts, bikini top and long-sleeved rash vest. I'm not a wetsuit kinda girl and the cold North Sea off Scotland isn't about to change that.

The tide is quite high, so I don't have too far to go to get in the water and it's as cold as I expected. I gasp as the huge waves envelope the still dry part of me and I gasp as my lungs attempt to acclimatise to the temperature. I get in far enough to be completely wet and splash about a bit, but I'm not a strong swimmer and the surf is strong.

That was fun!

As I clamber back to shore, a few people make passing comments about the sea being cold. You may not be surprised to hear I was the only person in there. It felt great to have an ice cold dip, but I'm glad of our cosy van, our hot shower and the diesel heater.

I treat myself to a far longer and more luxurious shower than we usually have in the van. I spend time washing my hair, then sitting on the toilet in the boiling hot wet room warming up as the diesel heater pumps in. I get dressed in some warm clothes and we're ready to get back to travelling.

I'm planning to work today, so we've picked out Achininver Beach where we can enjoy a nice beach walk with the dog and I can work with a view. There looks to be a park up right above the beach, and all being well we can also stay there tonight.

The drive is beautiful, the road follows the sea to our right, meandering in and out of the coves. It's been a mixed bag with the weather, and we've driven through a few showers and seen a few rainbows along the way.

The road winds on, past little stone cottages, and white painted houses, some with corrugated roofs, including one with a bright red corrugated roof that catches our eye in the distance. It's very pretty and puts me in mind of pictures of Norway I have seen in the past. For the first time on the trip we're seeing a lot of no camping signs and no overnighting signs now we've rejoined the NC500. We hope it doesn't prove too much of an issue.

The road winds inland and we now have mountains to our left. As we weave along the single-track road, we see a bird of prey over the peaks. It's low in the sky and it's flying towards the same point of the road in the distance that we're heading to. The camera is in the back, so we only have our phones. As Stuart remarks how big it is, using quite colourful language, we speed up a little in the hope of meeting it in the distance as it flies closer and lower to the point we're heading for.

Within a minute or so we've caught up with it, our first Golden Eagle in the wild. Does it get better than this? We follow it for a while before it sweeps off and back on itself but we're both utterly speechless.

Another tick off the wish list and despite not having the decent camera in the cab, the grainy photos still make me smile and I'm glad to have seen this majestic bird for myself. Stuart makes a mental note to keep the proper camera in the cab with us when we're driving.

We cut back towards the coast and we're looking out at blue-green seas and tiny islands and islets before us. As we come around the last bend, Achininver Beach comes into view beneath us and what a view it is!

The beaches along this stretch of coast are stunning white sandy coves with cerulean seas, broken up only by stretches of river pouring peat stained, dark coloured fresh water into the bays - although these oddly, offer their own beauty.

The parking space is a little pull in off the road, looking down to the sandy bay beneath us. The first thing we realise is that there is no signal on any of the three networks we juggle in the van, the first time in Scotland this has happened. Sod's Law! I'll worry about it after lunch!

I cook some brie and bacon wraps then we get ready to climb down for a walk on the beach. There are a few steps and a steep hilly trail to the beach, it's quite slippery and wet so we've gone for wellies. The cove is sandy with rocky sections along both sides. It's windy and cloudy pushing squally showers through. We toss the ball for the dog, and then make our down the right hand side of the beach, accessible due to the low tide and we climb over the rocks, exploring rock pools, tiny freshwater falls onto the beach and the beautiful pink rocks that make up the shoreline here.

It's rainbows aplenty and with every shower comes a fresh rainbow leaping out of the edge of the cove where the brown peat-washed waters meet the bright blue ocean waves. We walk back along the shoreline, playing with the dog, until we reach the river running down the beach and find it too deep to cross.

Dragging my mind back to the work situation, we decide we'll head back up to the van and find a park up where I can work. It's disappointing to leave such a stunning bay but needs must, and we have plenty more beaches yet to visit.

We get back to the van and Stuart gets a brainwave about turning the van around to boost the weak signal we have. As he spins it around, we lose everything, even our phone signal, laugh, and start driving to pick up a signal so I can look for the next park up on the map.

In the distance we can see an interesting looking mountain with several peaks, rocky protuberances, sharp escarpments, and challenging climbs. A ruined historic house called Moine House is marked on the map and it looks like it may have a parking area just off the A838.

It's only a couple of miles away and the signal is good in this area, so we make our way there, with the mountain to the side of us, disappearing in and out of view with the rolling weather. The park up is good, with perfect views of the mountain, that I now know to be Ben Loyal, views of Moine House, and across the nature reserve in between. There are signs in the car park directing campers to the nearest toilets and bins so we take this as permission to stay and get settled for the day.

We take a walk from the van out to Moine House and along the trail a little, but we don't get very far as it's incredibly windy. When we get back to the van, I sit at my laptop for a few hours and we end up having a static but relaxing day.

Several people come and go, including a large motorhome that blocks our view of the mountain for a while, and a lady car camping who is grateful of the shelter of our van to cook in. She's a travel writer and her and Stuart chat a while, allowing me to work and enjoy the view.

Stuart cooks and we have a quiet evening watching some television, listening out for aurora alerts, and discussing our poor luck for the solar storm forecast that has so far come to nothing. We're still hopeful but for now it's time for bed before another busy day tomorrow.

# Day 13: 2nd October

Compared to how blustery it was last night, and through the night, today is a lovely bright, clear day. The solo lady car camper who was alongside us last night is also up and about and we see her reorganising the car, from sleeping vehicle back into transportation. I spend a moment grateful for the big van and the work saved by having extra space.

We take some photographs of Ben Loyal in the clear light, discuss coming back to Scotland to climb it, and make a route plan that incorporates some of the North Coast's best beaches. We're soon ready to hit the road, so it's back out onto the main road from this little secluded car park and we rejoin the A838 and make our way back to the coast road.

This area is a treat to the eyes, the landscape is beautiful, both inland and out to sea. As we hit the coast, the road runs right alongside the sea, you could not be closer as the tide laps on a rocky shore less than a couple of metres from the side of the van.

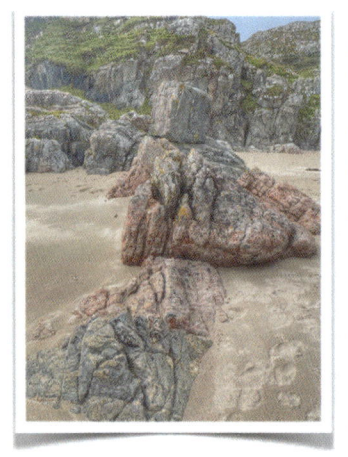

It's about twenty miles to our next location, Ceannabeinne beach.

When we arrive we find a small parking area just above a white, sandy bay, scattered with large pale pink rocks, and a river that follows the cliffs down the right-hand side of the bay. It's beautiful and more akin to what you might expect to find in a tropical location, the rust coloured, peat-stained water the only indication we are in Scotland.

We pull on our wellies, expecting a muddy walk down, and get going. We start to walk down and the river is as pretty as the beach. To our far right we see a tiny stone bridge and under it, the river crashes, tinkers, and trickles down a stony riverbed, over and between large pale grey rocks and down to the beach below.

We follow the freshwater all the way to the sea, one last hop down from the grass bank puts us on the sand. It's a windy day and the clouds remind us that autumn is never far away. It's fresh and blustery, whipping up the surf in the bay into big white waves.

As we walk across the beach we see a couple of surfers in the sea, fighting to master the huge waves coming into the shore. We watch them as we walk, swimming out then being brought back in on high-crested waves. A seal plays, just a little further out than the surfers, in the edge of the bay. They've seen it too and we watch them and it as they try and get a little closer to it. Eventually it disappears under the water.

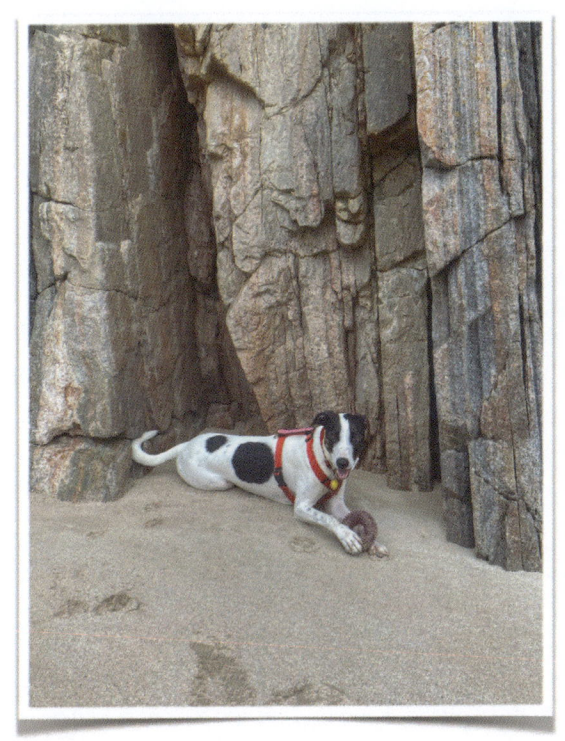

Alongside the dunes we stroll, watching grasses dancing in the breeze, to the other end of the beach. The far end of the beach is a huge cliff, sedimentary rock running at right angles to where it was first formed, creating narrow chasms of rock and crevices, in pinks, silver greys, and sparkling quartz, reaching up to the sky.

The sky suddenly gets very dark and we're deluged with a downpour, laughing and huddling against the vertical rocks for a bit of imaginary shelter. As the worst of it passes, we walk back along the bay, ready to dry off and get ready for the next location.

Lunch first. We didn't want to need to drive to supermarkets every day, so we packed a fair bit of food that won't go off. It's been quite a few days since our Tesco run and the fridge is looking a little bare. It's time to root in the big box we packed for the garage area under the bed. I dig out a couple of tins of soup and a pack of part baked baguettes and we demolish the lot, discussing how we should eat more soup in the van because that was a tasty lunch. Unsure if the soup is delicious or we're both just ravenous we mark Smoo Caves off as our next stop and get back on the road.

This area has lots of facilities including bathrooms, a large car park where you can stay overnight, and a Revolution Laundry. Despite how well facilitated it is, the caves aren't that busy, though there's lots of motorhome and van traffic in and out using other facilities.

We park up and make our way down the long steep steps to the cave, cross a bridge at the bottom and then catch sight of the huge, cathedralesque cavern before us.

There are Smoo Cave official tours, but they don't run every day and as they're not on today we make do with a look around. The cave is lit in such a way to highlight all the tiny caverns and nooks and crannies inside. We walk through the cave taking in all the delights, and follow the route over a tiny bridge along a wooden footpath into the noisiest bit of the cave so far. Inside, water is crashing down from above. What must be thousands of gallons of fresh, clear water, crashes down through a huge hole a great way above us in the top of the cliff.

Down it tumbles into a tiny chamber, which we are now standing in on a small wooden ledge. We are getting soaked, and the noise is deafening. It's quite the experience.

We walk around a little longer exploring, leave the cave and amble out onto the bay the cave sits in. We look around the stony bay, finding an old rusty boat winch, look for seals for a little while and then climb slowly back up the very many steps to the car park. It's still early but there's a change to the weather, squally winds blow through and as we are both cold and tired, we're ready to hit the road, another beach stop on the agenda.

We follow the coast road to Balnakeil beach, wind down the hill and pull up alongside the beach, a large house, and a ruined church stand sentinel one the shoreline.

The beach is beautiful, sweeping golden sands and dunes as far as the eye can see. There are several beaches here and we're planning a walk out onto the tiny peninsular alongside the Kyle of Durness, the other side of the poorly accessible Cape Wrath.

However, the weather has not improved and within a few minutes visibility is so poor we can barely see the beach. It's not the day for a scenic coastal hike and we call it a day and drive onto our planning evening spot, even though it's still very early in the day. As we drive to the Kyle of Durness, our planned overnight park up, I'm considering a hearty home-cooked meal to use up some of the hours left in the day.

The spot on the Kyle of Durness faces North but the predicted solar storm has been a damp squib and we're not hopeful. We're both a little disappointed, but did I tell you we saw a golden eagle? I guess you can't have everything.

We pull into the car park; a large flat exposed area right alongside the Kyle. There's indication that there's a cost for overnight parking in the summer but there's no one here to collect any cash so we dodge water-filled potholes deep enough to swim in and find a decent spot.

It's a lovely place, we ensure we're parked up against the wind, wrap up and head down to the shoreline for a walk with the dog. The weather is rough, but we clamber over rocks a while at the water's edge and brace ourselves against the gusts on the higher points.

I come back and start digging through the box of food for something fun to cook. We're almost out of fresh ingredients so I grab some dry soy mince, passata, some herbs and spices and ingredients to make fresh ciabatta and get started on a cooking afternoon.

Facing away from the wind allows us to have the door open as I cook, affording us of a perfect view of the Kyle, a narrow inlet of sea that we are currently watching empty out with the tide, exposing sand banks.

We had looked at visiting Cape Wrath, the most inaccessible north-western tip of Scotland but the only way to visit is via boat a little way up the Kyle from our park up and then a rocky old minibus ride out to the cape. It's also the only way to access the remote Kervaigh Beach (and bothy) but as the boat and bus doesn't run through the winter that was the end of that idea.

I make the ciabatta first and needing somewhere warm to leave it rest, it ends up locked in the shower room with the diesel heater on, not ideal but needs must in a small space. While it's doing its thing and rising, I make a spaghetti sauce with the soy mince, mushrooms and passata. The now risen ciabatta dough gets broken up and I layer it up in the bread tin, pouring on garlic butter between the layers. We don't bother with the spaghetti and scoop up the whole lot with the ciabatta, which has baked in a tear and share way and is easy to pull apart.

We're stuffed! Dinner was delicious. We've really pigged out so as the wind sways the van we decide to have a lazy evening and binge-watch something on Netflix.

It's starting to feel like bedtime when my phone pings. I glance over and see it's 11.30pm and there's an alert for aurora.

Oh!

The television goes off and we pull some shoes on and head outside. In the few minutes it's taken us to get ready another ping and the alert has been increased to amber.

It's been a really dreich day and it's not much better now; the sky is clear above us, but clouds hang toward the north. We stand and watch for a while and as the wind blows the clouds through, we see streaks of green and red through the gaps. We grab the cameras and get them set up on the picnic table, wrap up against the weather, I pour myself a (very) large single malt, and we stand watching the light show.

Seeing the aurora has been on my wish list for so long. Time after time I have dreamed of going to Iceland or Norway for the chance to see them. We've spent the first half of the trip gearing up for a solar storm that never came, and so I am thrilled to bits!

There's no denying the weather could have been better. We look at some pictures online taken over Shetland and Orkney where the skies are clearer and streaks of green and red ribbons dance across the sky. What we saw was more of a glow of light from behind the clouds, but I'm not complaining. We've ticked another thing off the list.

We keep watching for hours in the hope the sky will clear, and it's gone 2am by the time we retreat to the van, both slightly damp and cold, and me slightly tipsy from all the warming sips of single malt I've drunk while we watched.

## Day 14: 3rd October

It's almost 10am when we wake, which is hardly surprising given how late we were up. I'm stoked that we've seen the Northern Lights, just after we saw a golden eagle!

This adventure has been the trip of a lifetime and I feel as though we've been so lucky with everything, from the weather, which has brightened up considerably again today, to the wildlife. Yesterday was a gloomy day, today it's bright with brisk winds. We're going for a second attempt at Balnakeil Beach and the walk out onto the peninsula there.

We drive down to the beach and park in front of the imposing Balnakeil House. A large bright yellow house, you might think it would blend in with its sandy, dune filled surroundings, but this is a monolith on the landscape, more castle than house.

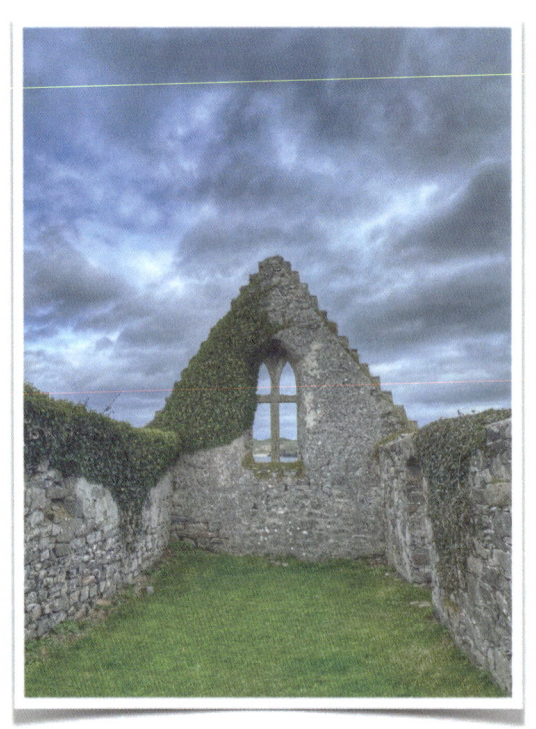

There are lots of no overnight parking signs on the seafront and it's little wonder as it seems to be a private house and then delicate dune structures. Behind us is a dilapidated church and graveyard so we go to look around before we start to walk and find the grave of Gaelic poet, Rob Donn. This overgrown, crumbling church and graveyard, sweeping out into the desolate, windswept bay makes me consider that there are worse places to spend an eternity. We take some pictures and head back out to the bay.

This long sandy peninsula is called Faraid Head, and strung out across several golden sandy bays, rocky outcrops, and gargantuan sand dunes it's unforgettably beautiful. It's a windy day but the sun is bright in the sky as we walk the length of the first bay, inspecting seaweed, shells, and stones as we go, tossing the ball for Nala.

The sea is clear and bright blue in the sunshine and the tall dunes to our right and in front of us are sparkling bright with the light of the midday sun. At the end of the beach the sandy path cuts between the dunes and we find ourselves walking between giant sand dunes, steep sandy sides loom twenty or thirty feet above us. The walk is beautiful, punctuated only by what sounds like military firing.

After a little while the sand starts to give way to grassy burrows. We can see cows grazing ahead so we put Nala on the lead and continue out onto the headland. There's another sandy bay to our left, we'll explore that on the way back. As we walk further out, we meet a couple and get chatting. They're here from Leicestershire doing the NC500 and they've spent the night alongside

Balnakeil House. We walk with them, sharing adventures until we get to the furthest point we can go. The path is closed, and from here we can see where the loud booms and crashes were coming from. The military are firing off the head over to Cape Wrath on the western tip of the North Coast. We watch a while as they fire, follow the sound, and then watch for the explosion over on the cliffs on the opposite side of the Kyle. It's quite the show, so when the couple we'd met head back along the path, we go off-piste and see how close we can get to the cliffs on the other side.

This tiny bit of land, jutting out to sea is stunning. We stand a while on the big cliffs watching the aquamarine waves crash beneath us and the shells explode on the opposite shore before walking back along the cliffs toward the second sandy beach we'd seen earlier. This beach requires a bit of a scramble down and as we descend, we see another big rusty boat winch like the one at Smoo Caves.

It's beautiful looking out into the craggy bay from this secluded beach, this has turned out to be the most picturesque coastal walk to date and it's hard to see how anyone could come here and not become a poet just like Rob Donn.

We climb back up onto the headland, back past the cows and back toward the gate to the dunes. A couple of military 4x4s come through and we chuckle watching the cows take advantage and push through the gap once the soldier has swung open the gate and gone back to his truck. After a small scuffle between cows and soldier, he's through, the gate is locked, and everyone is where they belong.

We retrace our steps, back through the dunes and back along Balnakeil Beach to the van, completing around 8km of delightful terrain.

When we went to Smoo a couple of days ago, we really should have done the laundry but neither of us really wanted to. We head back there now, pay for the car park and sit for a couple of hours using their Revolution Laundry. As usual Stuart takes charge of the chores and I catch up with some work on my laptop while the laundry machines do their thing.

We've only paid for a couple of hours parking, but they do allow overnight stays here. Once the laundry is done, we decide to press on and see if we can find a more picturesque park-up. It doesn't turn out to be one of our wisest decisions.

We're hoping to catch up with friends who live near Ullapool in the next day or two, but tomorrow we're heading to Stoer Lighthouse and the Old Man Stoer (not to be confused with the Old Man of Storr on Skye) so we're looking for a nearby park up. There's a village close by called Culkein and we can see a couple of spaces on the side of the road in on Google Maps so we drive that way and find one big enough for the van, on the edge of the cliff overlooking the beach.

The drive in is gorgeous, some of the most scenic roads we have travelled on to date. The view from our park up is spectacular, the rocky coastline giving way to chains of tiny islands out to sea. We are right on the edge, and considerably closer to the road than we'd usually choose. It's a quiet road so we're hopeful for a quiet night.

Over the next hour our view disappears as the sea fret rolls in and descends on the coast. Not long after come the winds, whipping around the head and out to sea, treating the long van, our tiny home, like a sail in the wind. We're settled for the evening, so we're resigned to stay.

We settle down and try and get some rest. I have a feeling it's going to be a long night.

## Day 15: 4th October

Well, that was possibly the worst night's sleep I have ever had in my life. The wind blew so hard that sleeping in the van on a cliff was akin to sleeping on a boat in rough seas, and when I wasn't being jolted awake by the van rocking, I was waking myself from scary dreams about the van rolling down the cliffs and into the sea. We're halfway through our trip now, and that was my least favourite park-up to date! Take our advice and stay in the overnight car park near Smoo Caves.

As rough as it was, there's no denying how scenic it is here and this morning it's bright, clear, but still blowing a gale, giving us a great view of this stretch of coast, the beach beneath us and the charm of islands just offshore.

First stop today is Stoer lighthouse and a sixty metre high sea stack a little way along the coast known as Old Man Stoer. We drive along the coast for a few minutes and pull into a large carpark in front of the lighthouse. With the standard white, yellow, and black paint job and the same stumpy style, it seems if you've seen one Scottish lighthouse you've seen them all, although the craggy outcrops and cliffs they stand on are ever changing.

There's a large sign up here detailing the marine life that can be seen from Stoer including grey seals, dolphins, and several species of whale. Maybe this will be the day I'll finally tick a great sea mammal from my Scotland wish-list.

We park up facing the sea, pull on our walking boots and waterproofs and get going. The waymark says it's 3km to the Old Man of Stoer sea stack and so we head in the direction it signifies across some very wet, slippery, boggy cliffs. The weather is changeable to say the least, just the drive over there took us through a couple of short showers, so we've come prepared.

The lighthouse is high on the cliff, we continue past it and drop down along the cliff path.

We come to a huge section where you can see the cliff has broken away from the mainland, shifting just a couple of metres. Judging by the life and growth in the chasm, this happened before the memory of any living person and we marvel a while at this rocky micro-ecosystem, created in this fault of nature.

The cliffs are beautiful, if a little muddy and we follow them along, in and out of the crags until we come to a beach beneath us. We don't go down as there's no obvious path, but we can see a waterfall dropping the entire height of the cliff down onto the beach, the wind creating an upside-down effect, blowing the water back up again. Navigating past it requires a few slippery hops, and it continues much like this along the whole cliff. Sea to our left, land to our right, and the run of freshwater channelling down to the sea across our path, every few metres or so.

Eventually, the sea stack becomes visible in the distance, a tall sentry standing guard in the ocean just off the protruding headland. With the wind whipping up around us, and the ocean crashing into heaps of white foam underneath us, the day is the kind you imagine described in a novel by Ernest Hemingway or Herman Melville.

It's loud, exposed, and unrelenting as we walk into the keen wind. We come to a small piece of land, stretching out to a rocky head, it's no more than an arete really, sea crashing either side of it, a meandering dirt path created by the daring. It's an invitation, and so I head out onto this exposed tiny, narrow isthmus and feel the full brunt of this northerly wind. We stop here for a little while, taking some pictures of the Old Man of Stoer, and scanning the sea for marine life.

We're visiting friends this evening, so we've been in touch with them throughout the day. They're about 30 miles away from here in a tiny village near Ullapool and it's already the middle of the afternoon so we decide to turn back and walk the couple of kilometres back to the van before hitting the next 30 miles of what looks to be winding, scenic roads through Assynt. There's a small ruined castle called Ardveck Castle just a few miles from where they live so we'll stop there first for a quick look.

When we get back to the van, we can barely see through the windscreen, the sea spray and salt fused on it by the wind. Back on the road and we're following a picturesque route the thirty or so miles to Ullapool. The road is beautiful, and mostly single track. Rocky hills undulate into the distance, trapping water in tiny inter-joined lakes and flow water either side of the road as we twist and turn through the landscape, watching imposing Munros grow as we get closer to them. The road opens out to a long flat expanse, bright orange bracken and bog myrtle give the scenery an autumn vibe. There's a carpark ahead for Little Assynt, just up on our left and as we pass it, I see a deer in the car park and tell Stuart. We decide to turn around and drive back and see if it's still there.

We pull quietly and slowly into the car park, watching the hind graze by the Little Assynt sign. She's aware we're here, but doesn't seem too bothered about our presence, so Stuart uses the van as a hide and gets some amazing close-up shots of her. We're ten minutes in before we realise she has a small fawn with her as it lifts its head from the long grass.

They're both adorable and we're glued to the spot for longer than we intend to be as we watch her and her calf. After about twenty minutes she heads off into the distance, and we also better get on the road, as we have plans..

Next stop, Ardveck Castle, which Stuart has been calling Aardvark Castle all the way here, to much amusement. This small romantic ruin is out on a grassy outcrop on the edge of Loch Assynt, adjoined to the land by a narrow strip of path. One finger of fortified rock and a single windowed wall is what remains of the castle, standing as a reminder of how imposing it must once have been.

Originally, back in its heyday in around 1490, Ardveck Castle was a three-storey tower house of traditional design, which included a corbelled section that once housed the main staircase and part of the vaulted basement level.

After a look around the ruin we head back to the road and cross to find Ardveck Falls, a tributary to the loch. It doesn't feel like much of a feature as it's slightly obscured, but this 30-foot, noisy, thundering waterfall is worth a look.

We've loved the remoteness of the trip, many places we've visited have been completely devoid of people, but it makes a refreshing change to meet with friends. John and Heather live in a beautiful, secluded cottage, surrounded by Douglas firs, a little way from Ullapool. It's impossible to tell where their garden ends and the countryside begins, which we think is perfect. Stags are a regular visitor to their garden, and from their window seat you can watch the mountains appear and disappear with the weather.

We get the loveliest welcome, and a full meal laid on. What an absolute treat! We have hot smoked salmon, sourced locally and I can honestly say it's the best salmon I have ever eaten. Heather has laid on a lovely meal with a bunch of sides to ensure there's something everyone likes, and we spend a delightful evening talking nature, politics, life, and the universe, over a very, very many single malts. John tells us how he came to Scotland and why he loves it so, we all discuss the languages of the United Kingdom for a little while, touching on Welsh, Scots and Doric, and Heather and I chat for a little while over our love of literature.

Nala plays a while with their two spaniels, but before long she's overwhelmed with all the fuss, and we leave her to sleep in the van.  By the end of the evening, I am a little drunk, and feel very intellectually fulfilled in the way that you do when you spend an evening in fine company. Stuart doesn't drink, so he's always designated driver, for which I am very grateful. Eventually I stagger back to the van, much to Stuart's amusement, find a layby on the A835 and I fall into bed.

## Day 16: 5th October

So, this is it, more than two weeks in and we've hit the West Coast of Scotland.

Our intention has always been to save the best until last, including a 'holiday with the road trip' on the Isle of Skye as we wend our way down the coast. Unsurprisingly, I've woken up with a dry mouth and a slightly thick head. Coffee is needed before anything happens today. Stuart mentions a supermarket run as we're so close to Ullapool, and I groan.

Refuel stop first then, both for the diesel tank and the fridge. We pop into Tesco and pick up some shopping for the next few days, including more beef olives (yum!), leave via the filling station and then we're off. We're not planning too strenuous a day, we had a late night and I have a hangover, though I'm at pains to admit it.

John and Heather recommended a local gorge walk, Corrieshalloch Gorge National Nature Reserve so that's first on our list today.

We arrive to find plenty of car parking at the side of the road, and a gate down to the trail for the gorge walk. It's a grey, murky morning but waterfalls lend themselves to wet days so we grab our raincoats and get going. As we zigzag down the trail towards the river, we explore the pine and birch forest around us, seeking out mushrooms, taking pictures. I find a few large boletus, and what looks like it may be a type of oyster mushrooms on a fallen log, so I collect a few up hoping to confirm identification later.

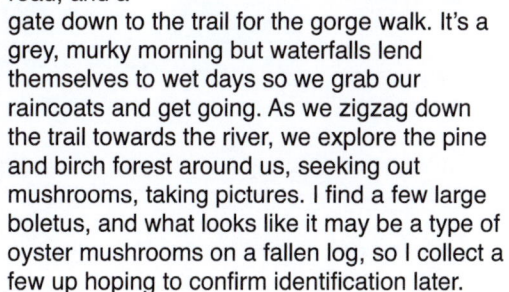

Eventually at the bottom of the trail, we come to a bridge crossing high over a deep ravine. From the middle of the bridge, the view is out of this world as the waterfalls crash beneath us over rocks smoothed by the passage of this water over thousands of years. Water tumbles down the gorge sides from all directions, creating a lush, green landscape.

On the other side of the bridge the path continues to the viewing platform. Sadly, this is made from that metal gridding we see often on coastal stairs; our dog cannot manage them with her small feet, so we take it in turns to stand out there and take in the watery, thunderous view.

We continue back up the path of this short and thankfully less strenuous walk and make our way back to the van. We've picked a spot about 30 miles south of here to end the day and it's a scenic drive so we're off again, Stuart driving while I do a little mushroom identifying as we go.

We drive a few miles and then spot a huge waterfall just on the left at the side of the road, there's a layby about 20 metres ahead so we swing in and park up so we can take a look.

We leave Nala asleep across the front passenger seats, adventure dog in rest mode, and walk back along the road to the falls. This may just be a waterfall on the side of the road, but it's one of the most impressive falls I have ever seen. We stand and look over the railing as the torrent of water crashes down its stony steps, creating mist and tiny rainbows in the light. It's loud, and we're getting wet from several metres away.

Stuart notices a muddy trail up the left-hand side of the waterfall and so we start to climb upwards, following this river, gaining elevation as the water crashes down the hillside much quicker than we could ever walk up it.

Waterfall after waterfall greets us, huge rocks, crevices, and shelves of rock send thousands of of gallons of water down towards the road. The ground is very slippery and boggy but it's so beautiful we keep heading upwards to view each level of the falls.

At one stage in history, a huge round boulder has been washed down the river and stands jammed between two rocks. At low water levels this would make a great spot for ghyll scrambling, combining scrambling with water for a fun adventure. Not today though.

We stand on the stone plateau, flattened through time by the passage of water but dry today, enjoying stunning views over the West Coast, salmon farms, tiny farmhouses with bright corrugated roofs, rugged coastline following the fjords and lochs in and out of the land.

It's cleared up to be a lovely day, offering visibility for miles and we just stand for a little while taking in the beauty of the coastline.

It's quite slippery climbing back down to the van, which makes for a fun descent with giggles aplenty. The dog is fast asleep when we get back to the van, this trip has been such an adventure for her, but she only has two modes, fast or asleep. We've found a park up on the apps and we're heading along the A832 alongside Little Loch Broom when we see it to the right of us and turn in.

It's a decent sized car park, flat, and the view is amazing. There are also bins and picnic tables here. It ticks all the boxes so this is where we're spending the night.  We got lucky with all our Scottish park ups, but there were a handful of stops that were unforgettably beautiful and this is one of them.

I cook with the door open, watching the view. Sadly, my mushrooms did not turn out to be oysters, but Angel Wings. I'm unfamiliar with these as they only grow in the North of England and Scotland so it's interesting to find them. They are eaten in much of the world but can cause kidney issues in people with known problems, so we err on the side of caution and give them a miss.

We're facing the North Coast and we're very near a campsite called Northern Lights Camping so we're hoping we might get an alert tonight; it never comes but we have a delicious dinner and a lovely relaxing evening in this beautiful scenic location.

## Day 17: 6th October

We've meandered along much of the route, winging it as we go, deciding day by day where to visit from our map of destination days. However, we're approaching the Applecross Pass, and particularly the Bealach na Bà – the Pass of the Cattle. It's one of the most famous mountain passes in Scotland, probably in the whole of the UK. The pass is one of the most scenic routes in the country, a zigzagging, steep mountain pass with many narrow switchbacks on the way down.

The road is closed in icy or snowy weather but we're still on the right side of winter so we're going to drop down the pass toward the coast. However, it's raining today, a lot, and we are in a large and heavy vehicle.

We don't feel it's ideal to do the pass in torrential rains and winds. Wet, oily roads could be a disaster for us, and we're hoping to climb a Munro once we get to the bottom, so a dry day is preferable. We spend an hour checking weather and maps and creating a route. Tomorrow looks the best weather wise, so we decide to head to the coast, take in a waterfall, and end the day at Applecross Sands, just before the pass.

A few people pulled into the car park overnight but it's still not very busy here. Our first stop today is Gairloch Beach (Gaineamh Mhòr), a sweeping expanse of sand about 25 miles away. It's another scenic drive. It's really worth saving the West Coast until last.

The beach car park is alongside the church in Gairloch and the spaces are plenty big enough for us. We pull on our boots and head for a walk down towards the beach, there's a small path from the car park alongside the church that takes you through the dunes and down onto this golden sandy bay.

The tide is out, creating miles of sand. We stroll down the beach in the midday sun, throwing a ball for Nala, enjoying the view of sandy bay, rocky coastline and little tidal islets with their own private sandy beaches.  When we get to the other end we find we can follow on through dunes and woodland to Gairloch Harbour so we carry on walking. It's a short but brisk walk over the hill and through woodland until we reach the downwards path to the harbour. We're expecting fishing boats and industry but what we find is a picturesque little hamlet where the residents clearly go the extra mile to make the place special.

The edge of the harbour, from end to end, has been turned into a long, narrow sitooterie. There are tables and chairs, benches, boats, all painted in vibrant colours.

Coloured flowers spill from raised beds at the water's edge, despite the lateness of the season, and painted quotes and messages dot the seafront. There's an art gallery and some little shops along the front. Toward the end is a toilet and a motorhome area with water, black and grey waste disposal for a small donation.

We're on foot, but it seems a shame not to make the most of this opportunity so we start the walk back to Gairloch Beach and the car park to pick up the van and drive back to the harbour to refill and refresh. I leave Stuart to do the jobs and walk up to The Gallery, where a husband and wife sell art, prints and jewellery. He is the artist, and she makes the jewellery. I look around and chat to her for a while pleasantly surprised at how reasonably priced all the art is. I buy some Highland Cattle Coo prints for my daughters and go back to meet Stuart who is all finished. Loo empty, water filled, we head off again for a waterfall less than ten miles away, just as it starts to rain.

We pull into the car park to Victoria Falls in Achnasheen just as the heavens open, and we're not the only ones. Like us, several couples are sitting in vehicles, looking out at the rain, and questioning their life choices as the downpour bounces off the gravel in front of us.

Thankfully it eases off after about ten minutes and the falls aren't too far from the car park, so we make a quick dash along the path. It's only a short walk to the feature so it's a convenient little stop to break up the drive today. There are a couple of viewing platforms to the falls, we wander along, take a few pictures and head back to the van. I'm ravenous so before we move on, we have some wraps for lunch.

It's a sensible move as the next stop is Applecross Sands, ready for the Applecross Pass tomorrow, which is almost fifty – very scenic – miles away. We weave through the countryside in our little home, taking in the views, glad to be inside as the weather sweeps in bring rain, winds, and hailstones.

The park up at Applecross is on the edge of military land. We pull up onto a large, flat gravel area with a view of Applecross Sands before us. It's almost dark already and the weather hasn't improved so we write the rest of the day off, I sit and catch up with some work, Stuart tidies up the van, taking advantage of the bins in the car park, and cooks dinner.

The evening disappears and we watch the moon rise, illuminating the barely visible bay before us..

# Day 18: 7th October

The weather is a lot more bearable today!

We're up early, excited for both the Applecross Pass and our hike. We're hoping to climb Beinn Bhan today when we finish the pass, it's one of the Munros clearly visible in people's pictures of the pass and I love the idea of not only conquering the pass, but one of the surrounding hills too.

It's just a couple of miles from here to the start of the Applecross pass so we get ready and head off. We approach the start of the pass, you know you're there as there's a big sign. The road here rises to a height of 2053 feet with gradients of 1 in 5 and hairpin bends, and is not recommended for learner drivers, or large vehicles or caravans after the first mile. The sign sits above a gate, there to close the road in adverse winter weather, and another sign offering an alternative route. We've pulled over to read it, and take some pictures and as we get ready to move on, I spot a stag in the field to our left.

However, it's not one stag, it's two and they are walking in circles around each other. We park up a little more safely and Stuart unpacks the camera to take some photos. We watch for twenty minutes or more as these two stags lock antlers and rut, the stag on the left forcing the smaller stag on the right to the floor, over and over. They go round for round, locking antlers, pushing heads, staring eye to eye as they battle for the greatest prize, the herd of hinds grazing quietly in the next field. The pair of stags are no more than twenty metres away from us and I feel like we have front row tickets to the greatest show of nature I have ever seen. Eventually, after one particularly brutal round, the smaller stag backs off and skulks off to the outskirts of the field.

I realise we haven't spoken for ages. I look at Stuart and we both have the same crazy grin on our faces. WHAT A SHOW!

Behind him I see, on the roadside, just two metres away from us, an huge, older looking stag watching us with the same enthusiasm we've watched the rut. We have no idea how long he's been standing there, silently on the roadside watching us but it's as though he's posing as Stuart clicks picture after picture of his majestic beauty.

I am speechless. How will anything ever top this?

That was an unplanned but very welcome distraction, we pull on ready to face the pass. The first section of the pass is a windy, upward road from Applecross, climbing higher and higher, winding through the hills. The roads are narrow, the corners tight, our van long but Stuart navigates this difficult road with ease all the way to the first feature, the Bealach na Ba viewpoint at 2053 metres. The viewpoint promises views across Scotland, it's started to rain; we can't see 20 metres off the hill. Isn't that always the way?

Thankfully the weather is passing through and blue skies prevail because as we wind, switchback after switchback down the other side, the views are out of this world. Huge, dramatic Munros rise either side of us, the endless coastline, seas and lochs beneath us as we traverse this small peninsula one hairpin bend after another.

About halfway down there's a small area to pull over, one of the only ones that isn't a passing place. We get out to take some pictures and notice that the brakes are smoking, not steaming, but actually smoking. They weren't joking about heavy vehicles! We let the brakes cool down as we take in the views and attempt to work out which of the surrounding Munros is Beinn Bhan, our hike for the day.

It takes us a while to work out where we'll park for the hike, so we came down the pass and then turned and started climbing it again before eventually pulling over alongside a waterfall to cross land and join the trail up Beinn Bhan.

Originally, we'd marked off a horseshoe walk, incorporating Sgurr Ghaoiachain and Beinn Bhan. Sgurr Ghaoiachain is the huge, imposing, rocky round top to the left as you come down the pass, Beinn Bhan sits behind it to the right of the horseshoe.

Given how changeable the weather is we've already discussed it on the way down and we've decided just to attempt Beinn Bhan (896m), to the peak and back, an 11km hike.

We get set in waterproofs and pull on our boots and start our walk. There are no paved trails here so we're following a route on OS maps, and it takes very little time before we're ankle deep in boggy ground. We've barely started the ascent when it begins to rain, and with it comes a howling wind.

Above us, both Beinn Bhan and Sgurr Ghaoiachain appear and disappear as the weather blows through and the conditions make for pretty tough going. As we ascend the ground becomes more uneven and we're required to scramble up some rocky shelves to gain elevation. You'd hope as we got higher the ground would get more solid, but no such luck and I'm very glad I have my poles to assist my balance against the holes, ditches, and watery tracks cut through the hill. We keep climbing and when the clouds are on our side, the views beneath us are spectacular.

They say when you visit Scotland not to worry about the weather, because if you don't like it, there'll be something different along soon, and they're not wrong. The wind brings sunshine, squalls, clouds, and blue skies, but it also brings me earache and difficulty balancing.

4km in and we're done. I'm soaked, my feet are drenched and my ears ache from the wind. My ankle hurts where I've turned it in a water ditch, and Stuart's waterproof gave up its intended purpose a couple of kilometres back. We remind ourselves we're on holiday and it's supposed to be fun and start the not-very-much-fun-at-all boggy hike back to the van.

I'm disappointed, but the lack of trails on many Munros makes for difficult walking and the weather isn't helping. Of the two peaks Sgurr Ghaoiachain looks like the best climb anyway, so we're promise ourselves we'll attempt the entire horseshoe on a future trip.

We're hoping to climb Nevis on the way back down the West Coast and increasingly I'm wishing we'd done it at the start of the trip. As Autumn marches on, undeterred by our plans, the weather is turning against us more and more. Failing a couple of unknown hills is one thing, but we really don't want to go home without climbing Ben Nevis.

The van is parked next to a small stone bridge so when we get back we dry off, get our wellies on, and climb down to explore the waterfall and river. It's very pretty, but while Stuart is enthusiastically playing with the dog and taking pictures, in all honesty, I'm fed up.

We don't know where we're going next. It's only lunchtime and we thought we'd be walking all day; the windy weather has me chilled to the bone and I'm in a bit of a funk. While we're discussing where next I decide I want fish and chips for dinner and this decision will lead us to one of the best park-ups all trip. I don't know it yet but there'll be plenty today to cheer me up.

We sit looking on Google for takeaways and decide we'll find a park-up for the night and we find a little takeaway based out off the beaten track near Plockton. It's about 25 miles away in the direction we're heading, so it fits the criteria.

We're a little confused by the Google listing. What is this? It's some kind of burger van/pop up takeaway, on a farm. It's called Off the Croft and the reviews suggest that they serve food they grow on the farm, the menu looks appetising, offering things like burgers, fish n chips, langoustine, and other local produce.

A couple of the reviews even mention staying near there the night at the airfield, and that there's a nearby coral beach. We're curious enough to want to check it out, so we find the strip of land behind Plockton airfield on the map, it's facing the sea, and looks like it might be a good place to spend the night.

I've already warmed up a little, which has improved my mood already. It's time to hit the road, head to Plockton and get some fish n chips in my belly.

The view on the drive is as pretty and scenic as any we've had during this trip, and while this story has focused on all our days out, these scenic drives offering panoramic view of the sweeping landscape have been some of my favourite hours.

It takes us just over an hour to get to Plockton and as we drive through the village, we navigate past little grass verges, and cottages, as highland cows and sheep graze on the side of the road. It's idyllic!

Eventually we come to a left turn down a farm track. We pull over on the verge and get out of the van to be greeted by around 60 turkeys gobbling at us from behind a gate, two collies in the yard, and the light coming from what seems to be the takeaway. We order fish and chips, and stand under the canopy while it's cooked, looking at other stuff on the menu and reading the notice about the farm to plate ethos here.

The strip alongside the airfield where we're planning to spend the night is just along the lane opposite, and is, we suspect, part of the farm that the takeaway is on. There are bins, a lovely sea view, and a small sign directing people down the path to a coral beach.

The sun hasn't yet set so we sit in the cab looking out to sea watching the spectacle, taking in the unique landscape Western Scotland has to offer and all the tiny little islands, crags, and rocks around the bay. I am not exaggerating when I say that this is the best fish and chips I have ever tasted in my life, and certainly the freshest fish I have ever eaten. The chips are home-cooked rough cut chips, the batter is light and crispy, and the fish tastes like it's fallen out of the sea and into the fryer. It's so good! There's way too much food, I usually just share a few of Stuart's chips but I have my own portion today and end up eating more than intended because it tastes so good!

It's still early so I sit and do some work for a couple of hours, then we route plan and decide what's next. The whole trip we've discussed a holiday within the roadtrip on Skye, it's Saturday tomorrow, and we're less than ten miles from the Skye Bridge, so this is it.

Tomorrow, the Isle of Skye. How exciting!

# Day 19: 8th October

Yesterday ended on such a high, the disastrous hike is all but forgotten. We're up and raring to go, ready to explore this nearby coral beach. We're assuming it's a beach that coral regularly washes up on, hopefully we'll find a piece! It's just along a track behind the van so we pull on our walking boots and head down the lane.

It's not just my mood that has lifted, the weather has also taken a turn for the better. The winds have died down and it's a sunny day, before long we're both feeling a little overdressed as we follow the half a mile track to the beach.

As we duck through the last couple of trees, the beach opens out before us and it's a jaw-droppingly beautiful expanse of white appearing before us. We drop down onto the beach, and we finally understand the meaning of coral beach, there is no sand here, everything beneath our feet, every inch of this white bay, is made of coral. Tiny little pieces of coral, mixed up with the teeniest whelk and cockle shells I have ever seen. Every inch of beach is like the perfect macro lens photograph. It's like nothing I have ever seen before, and I am mesmerised!

I feel like I can hardly explain how beautiful it is, these tiny pieces of coral under our feet. The closer we get to the shoreline, the bigger the pieces of coral until we are picking up pieces a few inches in size. I'm not sure if coral beaches are common elsewhere in the world, but I have never seen anything quite like this. It's remarkable.

The beach is a picture-perfect little bay, and just off it through crystal blue, clear waters are several tiny little islands, each with their own beaches and vegetation.

The beach is a bit of a contrast, white coral and shells meet black rocks covered in vivid yellow/green seaweed making the scene look like an oil painting, scraped out with a palette knife by an artist with heavy hands and a limited colour palette.

Stuart gets the drone out and is standing up on a rocky protuberance setting it up. Nala has got better with the drone since the day two incident, but hates the bit where it takes off, so I take her off with me to the far side of the beach and we go exploring. We have a lovely clamber around the cliffs, going out beyond the grassy head and back in again. It's so warm, I've long discarded my coat on the beach and I'm walking in a t-shirt. What a difference to yesterday. It feels like late summer again.

We're both hungry so we decide to make our way back to the van for a spot of lunch before we head off to the Isle of Skye!

The Skye Bridge is on the Kyle of Lochalsh. There's a Co-op just before you cross so we pop in and grab a few bits of shopping. It's not a huge store, but it's sufficient.

We come to realise pretty much every shop on Skye is also a Co-op and none of them are cheap, both food and fuel is cheaper before you go over to Skye. The bridge itself is a bit of a non-event really, you just realise you're on it and then you're on Skye. I bet it's exciting coming over here on the Skye ferry, but this is by far the easiest and most convenient way to get to the island.

Our first stop is Sligachan Old Bridge, it's where everyone seems to come first when they arrive on Skye as it's the first thing you see. We park up in front of the hotel and shops. There's a wedding taking place at the hotel, we peer in as we pass and then cross over the road towards open country, a huge bronze statue, and mountains.

A sign tells us the land is managed by the John Muir trust. The sizeable bronze statue was created by local artist Steven Tinney and is a sculpture of Norman Collie and John Mackenzie, two Skye climbing pioneers who first climbed and mapped the mountains in our view, the Cuillin Hills, or the Cuillin ridge, as it is affectionately known by climbers.

The ridge is known as the holy grail of British scrambling.

When the ten hardest British or Scottish scrambles are listed in order of difficulty, peaks on the Cuillin Ridge regularly make up more than half the list. All sources agree that the hardest climb in the UK is the Cuillin's Sgùrr Dearg and the Inaccessible Pinnacle, famously known as the Inn Pin, a 50-metre pillar at the top of a 986-metre steep, rocky scramble, reachable only with ropes and specialist equipment.

It's the Cuillin Ridge that makes up our current view. Clouds blow through but the ridge is clear; a long, ragged, monolithic shadow on the landscape, obliterating the view in that direction. The hills have an outlier, a slightly easier to climb, separate hill that isn't part of the Cuillin Ridge but is part of the Cuillin Hills, Bla Bheinn, and we're hoping to climb it while we're here.

We enjoy a lovely lowland walk along the river, taking all this in. Scotland has never looked so orange, it's like someone sprinkled Autumn over everything. It's very busy here though. We've seen more people in the last couple of hours than we've seen since we climbed Ben Vorlich back at the start of the trip. It's also very gusty and we're back to the fierce rain and wind we left behind a couple of days ago.

Stuart has wandered off with the dog and I'm making my way back towards the road and the car park, taking one last look at this vast and unincorporated landscape. As I do, the wedding party must be leaving the hotel as there's a musician playing the bagpipes and I am struck by a moment of magic, a lump in my throat as I stand alone and listen to A Gift of the Thistle played on bagpipes as I look at a scene that is the very epitome of Scotland.

From here we take the A87, Stuart driving while I look for a possible park up for the evening. As we round a bend, a huge waterfall appears before us, we pull over into the layby to explore.

It's pouring with rain, so we hop out and run along the road to take some pictures. We don't know it now but we'll drive past this falls several times over the next few days and thanks to an incoming weather system, it'll be bigger and more dramatic each time.

I've looked on the apps and there's a sea facing park-up down an old dead-end road just past the Old Man of Storr. The weather is giving me concerns for a night on a cliff. We've been here before! Still, it looks like the best spot for miles.

All the car parks here so far either have height barriers, or no overnighting signs, and lots of them are pay and display.

You can see the Old Man of Storr from miles away as you drive up the A87, even on this murky day. The low cloud is swirling along the ridge that the Storr is part of, and this ethereal mist combined with the surreal landscape makes the drive look like something out of a fantasy movie.

We're hoping to do the Storr tomorrow, for now we're planning to be parked up and settled down for sunset. We see the little track on the right and turn down it, check out a few spaces before we decide where to park and that's us settled. We should be looking out to the Isle of Raasay but you can barely see a thing, the sea fret obscuring the view completely.

Thankfully it's the best internet signal we've had on Skye so far so I settle down to work for a few hours while Stuart cooks us a meal. Our first day on Skye was fun, if a little damp.

## Day 20: 9th October

What a wild night! I thought the last cliff stop was windy, but I feel like we've been parked sideways into a hurricane. The van has been rolling in the gusts all night, like a sailboat over rough seas. It's still very, very windy this morning.

The Isle of Raasay still isn't visible, the mist is so heavy we can barely see the sea just a few metres away off the cliff. We're hoping the weather will improve soon as our plan is to climb The Storr to the top, passing the Old Man of Storr on the way up. The Storr is a rocky hill with a sharp face displaying several landslip features such as the Old Man of Storr, and the other spiky pinnacles on the hill.

We're not in any rush to do things today so we hang around waiting for the weather to lift. I decide to grab my laptop and get on with work during the downtime and the day pretty much slides by in a few hours of heavy rain, howling wind, and me tap, tapping on the keyboard.

We're both fed up by late afternoon and we decide we'll head to the Talisker Distillery for a look around, where it will at least be dry.

Originally, we were planning to do a distillery tour, but we didn't want to book in advance and tie ourselves indoors on what might have been a dry day. The problem is the distillery gets booked up months in advance. Even this late in the season it's booked up until the last week of October.

They have a store and a bar that is open to the public, so we head over there to see what they stock. I'm hoping to get to taste some of the more expensive blends at the bar! I've already bought a large bottle of the standard Talisker on offer at Tesco in Ullapool though, as this is much cheaper than the on-site shop.

It's quite a drive across the island to the distillery, the weather isn't great but it's still beautifully scenic with the views across the land, and sea afforded from this small island. The distillery has a huge car park, and over this way there's also toilet and shower facilities in an area just outside the distillery, though you'd need to pay. We're discovering that very little is free on Skye, even parking.

The shop is what you'd expect from any gift shop, and it's the place to go if you want to ensure you pay top price for Talisker. If you just want a bottle of Talisker, the supermarket is cheaper, but they do have lots of other items in the shop that you can't just buy anywhere, including special blends and aged versions costing up to £400 a bottle. I'm keen to try at least a shot of one of these amazing, aged versions, which is really all I've come here for. The bar is visible from the shop, though there's no one in there. It's a stylish corner bar in the other end of the building with plush barstools, bench seating, and a real flame fire giving the whole place warmth.

I pick up a small gift bottle of Talisker as a souvenir for a friend and we go to pay. While we're at the counter I ask the young girl serving how we order a drink from the bar and she tells me the debit card machine isn't working in the bar. I respond that I'm happy to pay cash and I'm keen to taste one of the £400-a-bottle versions, but she just shrugs and replies that it isn't working. She's probably paid minimum wage, and I'm not criticising her, but I feel Talisker missed a trick here. If you want people to pay £400 for a bottle of single malt, you surely must appreciate that someone is paying for an experience and the chance to talk to a knowledgeable member of staff and be able to experience the drinks.

This is the only commercial thing we've done all trip, and it's reminded me why we do so little of this kind of thing. The whole Talisker experience left me feeling a little flat. It was disappointing to find we had to book more than a month in advance for the tour, and then to have a poor experience when visiting too left a poor taste, and not the taste of £400-a-bottle single malt!

Today hasn't been the most fun day, too much rain, too much work, and not enough fun. It's not really Scotland's fault, I suppose a whole month of perfect days would be too much to ask for.

It's only mid-afternoon, so there's still time to save the day! Stu has found a potential park-up alongside the river.

We leave the Talisker Distillery via the B8009, follow the road a little way before taking the second small turning on our left, along here a little way we have marked what looks like a small, circular park-up by the Eynort River on the map. When we get there it's perfect, offering stunning views down to the river, and across the countryside until the eye hits the Cuillin Ridge.

It's stopped raining so we take a quick clamber down to the river and follow it for a little while. It's not the kindest terrain, but it's nice to get out and get some fresh air and it lifts my mood considerably. We're back at the van before sunset and end the day with a meal and a relaxing evening. We're holding out for better weather for the Storr tomorrow. Attempt two coming up.

# Day 21: 10th October

That was a lovely peaceful park-up, we didn't hear a peep all night and we were sheltered from the wind too. The weather does look to have vastly improved today, which means breakfast and then the Storr walk! The Old Man of Storr is one of the most popular walks on Skye, we're hoping to pass the Old Man and continue up onto the ridge and climb the Storr too, making it a full hike.

It's late morning by the time we eat and arrive at the large car park at Storr. Like most car parks on Skye, it's pay and display, and the spaces aren't very long. There are limited van and motorhome spaces on the road, so we fill one of those and get ready to go.

It's one of those days – like most in Scotland – where you don't know what the weather will do in the next five minutes. We pack the bag, Stuart optimistically packing the drone, and get started on the steep climb up to the Old Man of Storr, one of several rocky pinnacles left behind by erosion on this hill.

It's very busy here. Scotland's kids are on half term this week so the whole island is quite busy; although I suspect it's always busy on Skye. However, despite the crowds, it's hard not to be captivated by this enchanting landscape.

The views surrounding us look like they've come out of the imagination of Tolkien and once we've gained some elevation, we stop to take some pictures. You can see the coast from almost every vantage point on Skye and this is no different, the sea before us looking moody and rough today.

Loch Leathan is beneath us with its rugged, uneven shape offering a magical feel to the landscape, and the pinnacles that make up the features on Storr all around us. The contrast between the lush green grasses and jagged ebony rocks is striking, and this undulating ragged landscape is breathtaking. To add a little extra magic, there are mountain hares everywhere! Nala spends the whole walk on high alert.

We follow the narrow dirt trails all the way up to the Old Man of Storr, the final climb right up to the rock proving a little tricky. The rock is huge and until you're

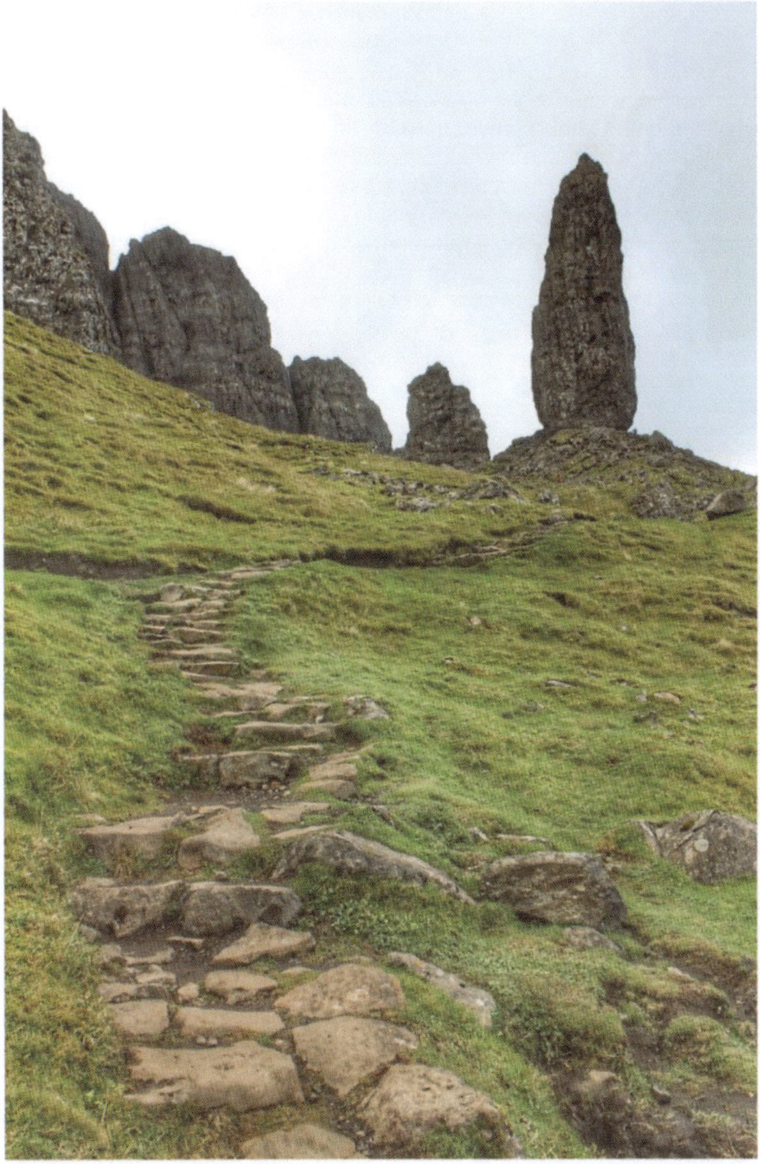

standing alongside it, it's hard to appreciate just how vast it is, standing here impossibly and precariously on a mountainside.

We're planning to pass the Old Man and continue climbing to the Storr, but there are workers here laying new paths and it means the path to the peak is closed. It's the first time I've ever tried to climb a mountain and found it closed!

It's a bit disappointing. We were really hoping to reach the peak. There are other paths, but you can see the are being re-laid to prevent erosion and with little signs asking people not to further erode the paths, we do the responsible thing and make our way back down, enjoying the broad views of the ridge and coastline. The drone did not come out all walk, unfortunately the weather on Skye has not been great and the winds especially have worked against us.

As the hike was much shorter than planned, there's still a few hours of the day left. I sit and look at the map and all the places we've tagged and we decide to drive from here over to Kilt Rock and Mealt Falls viewpoint. Mealt Falls is a long drop fall that crashes down the cliffs and into the sea and it's just nine miles from here.

It's incredibly windy when we arrive, and busy! The viewpoint is only a few steps away from the car park so we leave Nala sitting in the van in the warm and walk out to the viewpoint. It's so busy we must wait our turn to take a photo, it is beautiful though and it's clear to see why there are so many people here.

The water thunders down the cliff face, the recent rain helping to ensure we get the full effect. You can't get near the falls, but there's a specific viewpoint where you get a great vantage of them. I head back to the van, but Stuart decides to take the drone up to see if he can get a better shot of the falls. It's on this footage that we can see the loch, thundering river, and then waterfall in all its glory.

I can hear him outside in full conversation with a photographer about the drone and the best ones to buy, as Nala as I sit quietly out of the weather taking in the coastal view.

An Corran Beach is just three miles up the road, one of the few places on Skye and in fact Scotland where you can see fossilised footprints. Scotland's acidic peat heavy soil means that very few fossils have ever been found here but An Corran is the exception to this.

166 million years ago a group of meat-eating Megalosaurus walked through the mud here, next to a warm, shallow sea. Layers of mud covered the footprints and they were preserved as fossils. It took until 2001 before a dog walker found a footprint on the beach and since then palaeontologists have found seventeen footprints here scattered across the rocks.

The tide is right up when we get here and the sun is setting, there'll be no dinosaur hunting tonight. I cook and we watch the sea for a while. There are lots of campers parked up here and Stuart stops to chat to the couple in a motorhome next door who have spotted a seal in the water. They're travelling the opposite way around Scotland to us, so Stuart makes some recommendations to them, and we let them get on with their evening.

The parking spaces here are just inches from the high tide beyond the rocks and we fall asleep that night listening to the lull of the waves lapping up against the rocks.

# Day 22: 11th October

We're up before 9am after a peaceful night's sleep. The tide is out now and it's a bright clear day. This part of coastline is beautiful. The sand here is jet black, as are the rocks along the shore. Just off the mainland is an island, and a sign here informs us that this has long been summer grazing for cattle in the area, with the farmers swimming the cattle out and back at low tide. I wouldn't mind being here to see that!

It's time to go dino-hunting! We wrap up against the wind and make our way down onto the beach. A flat bedrock makes up one side of the beach and it's here where the footprints appear as the sand exposes them on the tides. We find one quickly and take precarious steps along the very slippery rocks looking for more. The footprints are cool, and we find a few more marks and indentations that we think could be further footprints in various states of completeness.

An Corran Beach fills up very quickly as people start to arrive to look for the dinosaur footprints for themselves. We walk along the glossy, ebony sand and rocks, take a few photos, chat with a few other tourists while the dog chases a ball for a while, and make the decision to move on.

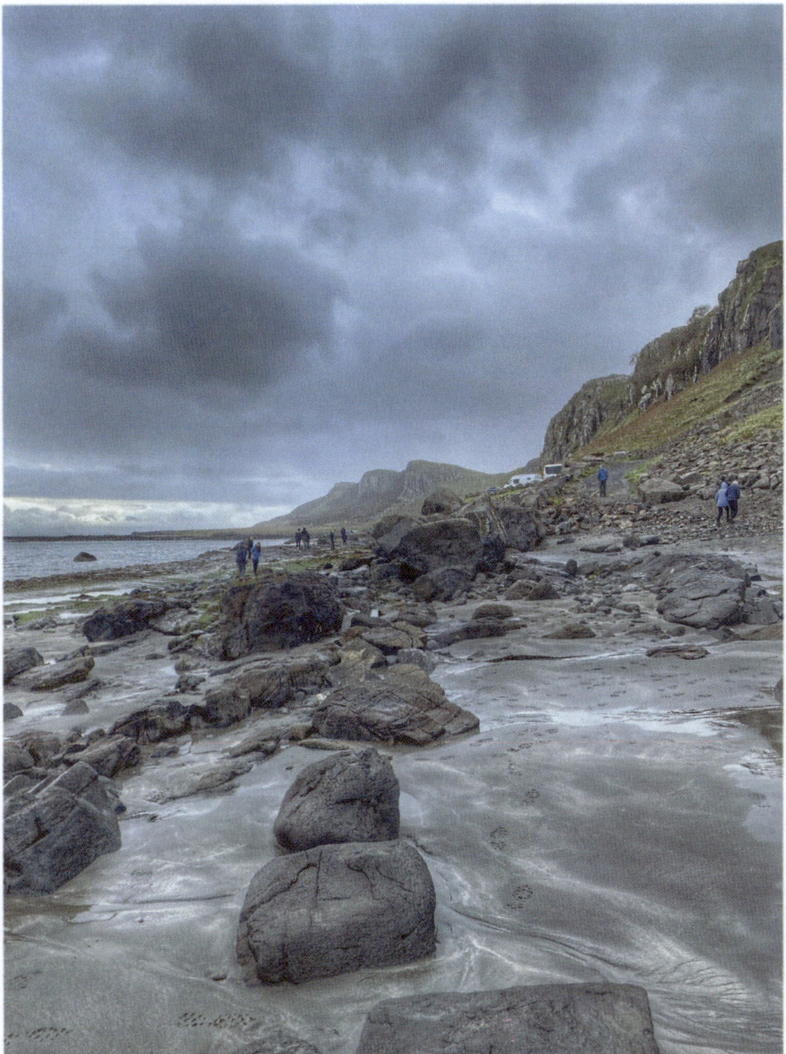

We need fuel so we stop at the Gleaner fuel station in Uig. There's a little shop too, and a nearby toilet block so it's a handy stop off. We fill up, and use the facilities, and I buy some little wooden Christmas decorations made on Skye for my mum from the shop.

This morning's brighter weather is a distant memory and rolling low clouds and showers scutter through.

Our next stop today is The Fairy Glen. It's described as a magical glen with various features created by landslips. There's roadside parking and like nearly all of Skye, it's pay and display. We pay for a couple of hours, pull on our waterproofs and get going.

It's such a dreary day with permanent drizzle and low cloud as we walk among the mounds across the landscape. Eventually we come to the rocky structure at the centre of the glen. This basalt hilltop looks like a ruined fort from a distance, giving it its name of Castle Ewan. It's slippery with the wet weather but we climb to the top and take some photos. From here you can see the fairy circle below, shown on many Trip Advisor reviews but the stones have been removed and it's not much to look at, just a muddy mess really.

Maybe it's just the terrible weather but I'm completely underwhelmed. The Fairy Glen has not enchanted me, and I'm a little wet and dreary. We make the most of it and walk the whole glen before heading back for lunch. We've paid for two hours so we eat here, I make us brie and bacon wraps, with the Scots brie we bought at the supermarket. They're delicious and as soon as I eat and dry out, I start to feel a little brighter.

The shop at the fuel station didn't sell much so we're heading to Co-op before we park up for the night, We pack down and close the cupboards and get ready to go shopping. Stu pulls off and heads down to the coach turning circle and as he turns there is a huge smashing sound from the back of the van. I have left a large Kilner jar on the bed and it's flung off onto the floor as we turned. There are tiny shards of glass everywhere!

We spend a while cleaning up, ensuring we've got every piece of glass and then make a very quiet drive to Co-op where we also do some shopping in near silence.

We're both feeling a little less joyous than usual, and we're struggle to find the enthusiasm for looking for an exciting park up. Someone on Facebook has mentioned that Loch Scavaig is a must visit so, with nothing better planned, we head there. I need to sit and get some work done so we're calling the day early anyway and as we drive around Loch Slapin with intermittent signal, I'm already concerned I won't have Internet for work.

We get to Elgol Beach, our planned park up, where we're absolutely battered by the winds. There's no phone signal, or Internet signal, on any of our three networks. I'm tired and want to settle down for the evening, but alas, this is not the spot. Elgol Beach looks like it would be a perfect place to visit and stay, but like much of today, luck doesn't feel as though it's on our side!

We're planning to climb Bla Bheinn tomorrow, which is nearby. I'm usually so excited the day before a big walk, trawling over the route, perfecting it in my head, but I just can't get excited and despite the forecast, the current weather is not suited to scree paths and slippery gullies.

Without much to say, we leave Elgol and drive back up the steep hill out of the bay. We drive a couple of miles back along the B8083, passing a few cottages and a farm until we come to a small flat area with a rocky face on the left. We have mobile signal, we can get far enough off the road so we're not rocking with the traffic. That'll do. We're calling it the end to what feels like a long day.

I sit and clear some emails, daily tasks, and freelance work as we're well into the new month now. I'm so lucky to be able to work on the road, but sometimes it takes more than a little discipline to kick my own arse and 'sit at the desk'. Today was one of those days.

We have a glut of wraps so I make us tortilla wrap pizzas and we pig out and watch some television.

# Day 23: 12th October

An early alarm shakes us from our sleep, and we wake to dry, calm, and bright weather, just like the forecast promised. All memories of yesterday forgotten, we're up for an early breakfast, excited to climb Bla Bheinn today. I eat muesli and fruit as I internally kick myself for not being more enthusiastic about my route planning yesterday. I quickly read over the route again, paying note to a section where if we reach a large boulder we've overshot the route according to Walk Highlands, and comparing it with the OS route I've marked out, which I think is a different route.

We pack up the rucksacks, double checking we have all our safety gear and we're covered for all eventualities, then hit the road back towards Loch Slapin and the Bla Bheinn carpark.

Skye contains some of the hardest mountain climbs and scrambles in Britain, and according to many respected lists and guides, as many as eight of the top ten hardest tops to bag in the UK are on Skye on the ridges belonging to the Cuiilin Hills. The name makes them sound meek, but with seventeen summits, the most brutal ridge on British soil, and Sgurr Dearg, affectionately known as the Inaccessible Pinnacle, and without a doubt the toughest summit in the UK, these mountains are not to be underestimated. Bla Bheinn is an outlier, offset from the main 'Black Ridge', but we're going prepared.

Boots laced, and a quick visit to the composting toilet in the car park here and we're ready to go. A few others have stayed the night here and there are three motorhomes in the car park when we leave the van. It's early and we understand this is likely to be a whole day's walking, so we get a good pace on to start, following the stone path over a bridge and up along the river, past cascading falls, and the increasing signs of Autumn all around.

We've climbed a little onto a flat section where the map says we need to cross a river. It is incredibly boggy, and it makes what should be an easy part of the walk, heavy going and strenuous under foot. We come to the section where we need to cross, and the water is flowing fast! It's easy to see where the rocks are that others have used, and erosion shows us where they stepped out the other side, but everything is wet and slippery.

A decision is made to walk further upstream, and we commit, but in truth by the time we had crossed, it would have been drier to chance the river. The land here is ankle deep in water in places and every step releases the scent of bog myrtle as we walk.

Thankful to be finally over the stream, we continue, dark rocky peaks loom above us as we snake left through the valley and climb what the map assured me was a path, but that felt very much like climbing a waterfall to me!

The route, a mixture of walking and small clambers so far feels gentle as we come to a grassy, flat opening between the hills. The clouds break and as the sun shines through, the whole area is flooded with sunlight, a kaleidoscope of verdant shades take my breath away momentarily. This kind of moment is exactly the reason I climb mountains and push through for big hikes. We decide to stop for a rest.

I walk ahead a little with the dog while Stuart gets out the drone to take some shots. The sky has cleared to reveal the most brilliant blue day with fluffy white clouds travelling slowly overhead. After the rain and gloom yesterday it's nice to take a moment to soak it in.

Ten minutes, and we're ready to go again. Now we're here I can see a huge boulder in front of us, my route will take us past it before we climb a scree bank. I realise that my route and the Walk Highland Route split here and we are going to walk past the boulder and along the sharper route. We're experienced but now I can see what is on the map in front of me in real terms, so to speak, it's clear we've picked a challenging route.

Undeterred, we continue and now the real climb to the summit is on. We're faced with a steep, scree bank up and with peaks towering above us, we know there's a long way to go yet. The scree is hard work, with every step forward there's a slide of several inches back and the bank is so steep it's hard going. I find myself walking in tiny zigzags to take a bit of the strain.

It's still early in the day though and we're both feeling energetic, we push on, laughing at the impossibility of the terrain and stopping regularly to catch our breath and take in the ever-improving view.

Eventually the scree starts to give way to slightly bigger stones and then rocks and here the route takes us around to the right and up through a boulder field. I let Stuart go ahead creating a gap to give me reaction time to any falling stones and seeing him above me really shows just how steep this route is.

There is no real clear path, but you can see on worn boulders, and in the tiny cairns that have been built on significant boulders, the way that others have gone before you. Trusting the cairns, I don't consult the map again. Slowly but surely, we pick our way to the top, although we're still a long way from the peak.

The route we've chosen requires us to walk around the top towards the trig, and there's a bit of a descent into a gully to navigate yet so we stop for a drink and then continue, glad to be on our feet walking rather than scrambling.

The views in every direction are so beautiful, I can hardly describe them. I can see the best part of the coastline of Skye, allowing me to see the island almost in its entirety. The main Cuillin ridge looms to one side of us, a craggy, rocky shadow, obliterating the view behind it. The Small Isles trailing out into the sea beneath us, the other side, the long island of Rassay snuggles into the side of the Skye coastline, and the mainland is clear in the distance. Every direction offers a different view of hills, rugged coastline, and ocean views, it's breathtaking.

The clouds pile up a little and as we reach the gully it starts to rain. What shows as a gully on the route looks more like a waterfall with sharp drops, sheer faces, and loose rocks and scree in what is a 150-metre chasm cut into the hill.

Thankfully the path back up to the peak on the other side looks more manageable, so we assess the descent, decide it's safe, grab out the long rope for the dog so we can allow her to proceed at her own safe pace, and we start to descend, rock by rock, lowering ourselves into the deep, wet, and slimy gully, one at a time so as not to tumble rocks down on one another.

As is usual with these things, it looks scarier than it is, most scrambles are not so hard when taken step by step and we're soon at the bottom ready to make the final climb to the peak. The weather is showery now, the bright sunshine gone and reappearing again as the clouds blow by.

It's a short, sharp ascent from the gully to the trig point but we're on it all of a sudden. We clear the last half a kilometre in no time at all and arrive at the prize, a little out of breath. There's another couple at the trig who had taken the Walk Highland route, they'd been watching us navigate the gully and we stand chatting for a while.

The weather starts to clear, and we sit on a boulder eating the ham and cheese wraps we brought up here with us. We stay at the trig for ages, and I walk along the edges of the mountain top, committing the awesome views to memory. With the sun high in the sky, Stuart gets out the drone and takes to the air, while I stand on the edge of a scree crevice, watching a rainbow that has plunged from the sky above me into this deep cavernous abyss between the two peaks.

We both start to get cold, and so we make our way down, taking the Walk Highland route back, rather than going back to the gully. I'm not sure either route was easier and with a couple of kilometres of steep scree path to descend, the least said about it all the better.

Soon we're back down on the flat, lush plateau between the peaks, and making our way back towards the river. We risk the river crossing this time rather than fight the boggy ground and despite much laughing and merriment, neither of us fall in. The descent takes no time at all and we are soon back in the car park where there are another couple of vans parked up for the night.

We decide to drive back to the coastal park up we used earlier in the week, with the intent of having one last walk tomorrow at the Quiraing before leaving Skye earlier than originally planned. The rest of the day passes in a blur and we hit the sack exhausted but feeling accomplished.

## Day 24: 13th October

When we planned this trip, we kept the plans quite loose. We tagged lots of hikes, features, and places to visit on a map and then we worked out the route by planning ahead just one or two days at a time. The only thing we've been fixed on since the planning started is that we wanted to spend at least a week on 'magical' Skye. We hoped our time here would be a holiday within a holiday in what is often described as the jewel in Scotland's crown, giving us time to take in the features and relax for a few days.

Skye has been beautiful and the places we've visited have mostly met our expectations. However, it hasn't been the chance to kick back and relax like we thought it would. There are a LOT of people here, and all the car parks are geared to daytrippers, making it very hard to find a spot to just kick back. So, we've decided to have one last walk today, then we're going to skip the Fairy Glen, after all, could you beat Puck's Glen from the start of the trip for a waterfall walk?

We'll walk the Quiraing today and head back to the mainland, where we've decided to go back through Plockton just for another takeaway at Off the Croft, the only place we visited twice in our entire thirty-day trip. After all, the whole point of staying on Skye was to relax and what better way than a delicious home grown takeaway?

First the Quiraing!

It's so windy today, and we're both feeling the burn after yesterday's big walk, but we want to make the most of our final day so we drive to the Quiraing, pay the roadside pay and display fee and start to walk the narrow ledge along this landslip feature.

The brisk wind is sometimes hard to walk against, but it keeps the clouds flying through at speed, giving this lush, green landscape against the purple tones of the sky, an emerald brightness.

The path is a narrow track following the ridge line above it. The first section requires a bit of a clamber down some rocks, and then it's through a waterfall, well worn by centuries of walkers who have steadied themselves as they cross. We continue, the dog fixated on a mountain hare beneath us. Stopping to watch we find as you focus on one, another comes into view and before long we can see a dozen or more hares down the hill. Stuart gives Nala a tug on the lead and we continue, much to her chagrin, and we spend much of the walk trying to distract her from the animal life on the grassy banks beneath us.

It's quiet here today, the fierce winds keeping many away, but it's easy to imagine how busy these narrow mountain tracks get. We get to the end where we're completely beaten back by the wind. I can barely stand on my feet at the crevice at the end of the path as the wind pushes me off balance over boulders. We decide to turn back, hit the road, and make our way to the mainland for a quiet evening and some dinner. Neither of us is feeling overly energetic after yesterday's big hike so we make our way back to the van, my mind already on tonight's dinner.

We start the drive through Skye, the recent rain creating vermicular streams down the hills all around us until eventually we're over the Skye bridge and back to the mainland. As we meander back towards Plockton, we discuss our plan for the next part of the trip. browse the map and places we've tagged, and realise that really, we only have Arisaig, and then the Fort William area left to explore.

We're hoping to climb Ben Nevis but Autumn marches on with ever decreasing dry, clear days, and ever-increasing snow on Scotland's biggest top.

For the first time we wish we'd been a bit more organised, as it's clear that getting the ferry back would have put us right at Arisaig, the next place on our list. We'd have also got the experience the island ferry! We're already discussing coming back for a proper island hopping trip so watch this space.

We stop at the takeaway at Plockton. We spoke about this place earlier in the trip and how they take food from the farm to the takeaway on the premises. We had fish and chips last time, so today we both try the burgers, made from the herd of Highland coos that roam and graze around Plockton. Both the fish and chips, and tonight's burgers, are two of the best meals I have ever eaten.

Even writing this my mouth is watering, remembering the home-made chips, and the freshest, most flavour-rich burgers I've ever eaten. If you've read this far you've probably noticed, we don't eat out much, takeaways are a real treat, and Off the Croft in Plockton is a real treat!

We're parked up on the airfield again so we settle down and just spend the evening watching a bit of television and relaxing.

## Day 25: 14th October

The whole month has flown by, it seems impossible that we're in the final week of our trip. Our little travel map is almost covered in dots now, leaving just the Borders and Lothians to the East that we didn't dip into this trip, and everything south of where we are now, which is mostly west coast and Fort William.

After a lazy morning we get ready to head off for our next stop, Arisaig. We have a bit of a drive from Plockton to get there. We don't mind too much, we're on a road trip after all, and the drive turns out to be as picturesque as you can imagine.

The weather has brightened up again, showing off the colours perfectly as we drive through a kaleidoscope of yellows, oranges, and reds as the Scottish landscape displays her Autumn tartan. We meander down the coast, looking out to the unique rugged coastline here with its rocky undulations and strings of tiny islands, stopping a couple of times to take pictures. The landscape gets prettier and prettier, until we finally arrive at the stretch known as The Sound of Arisaig, and I am instantly blown away with its beauty, helped along by the bright, sunny day.

There's barely anyone here, and as we crawl along the coast in the van, we take in all the views along the Sound, the sun reflecting off the bright blue sea. Eventually we end up at a car park at Camusdarach Beach. There are strictly no overnighting signs here, but we'll worry about that later. We park up and head through the dunes towards the beach.

The dunes and burrows meander in little narrow pathways created by human activity, and we walk and chatter, the dog pulling ahead excitedly, aware she's at the coast.

Eventually the dunes open up before us, putting us on the sandy bank of a river flowing through the beach and down to the sea. It's an absolute feast for the eyes with sparkly silver sands in every direction, the sun reflecting off the bright turquoise sea here, so clear you can see to the bottom. We're on a long, sandbank, interconnected with rocky islands, covered in bright orange weed and all array of ocean flora growing over and between the rocks.

The sand here, rich in graphite, shines silver in the sun, and tiny beaches stand in between the larger rocks creating private little bays, magical coves, and rock pools.

We walk down the beach, both speechless at the beauty here, climbing up over the rocky sections, and wandering the shoreline looking out into the shallow, clear water.

The sun is shining, but it's cold, it feels like October and yet the view before us wouldn't look out of place on a tropical island. This is a reminder that the UK is an archipelago, as delightful to the eyes as any island chain around the world.

The seas here look so tempting, and by the time we get to the final beach, I'm cursing having not brought my swimming gear because I would love a quick dip. Stuart isn't a big wild swimmer, not in the UK at least, so it tends to be just me who has a swim.

Next thing I know, Stuart's daring me to skinny dip with him and we've stripped down to nothing and run into the sea. There's no one around, and we have the secluded bay to ourselves so why not? It's freezing. I mean icy, icy cold, and the warmth of the Autumn sun has done nothing to take the chill off.

For once Stuart is braver than me, going right in, lamenting the loss of his nuts, and dashing back out again. I make it just past my waist and run back out again screaming and laughing. The dog jumps about and is barking frantically at us. We stand laughing and shivering, pulling our clothes over our wet skin, not a hint of even a hand towel between us.

We're still laughing as we make our way through the string of beaches back to the van. A couple stop us to ask if they'd seen us skinny dipping, we confirm, and set off laughing again.

We're both cold so we get back to the van and decide to find somewhere to stay for the night. It's midweek so it's quiet here, and it's out of season. This late in the day we find we're the only ones here, so we don't feel too bad about parking up alongside the beach on the verge.

There are very few places to park here in Arisaig and in hindsight, this is the kind of place you'd probably need to get a campsite 90% of the time, especially during high season. We've got lucky though so we decide we might as well make the most of it.

After a quick warm in the heat of the van, and some dinner, we decide to make the most of the sunny evening and get a fire going. We carry a firepit everywhere we go so we can leave no trace, and we've got a stack of firewood in the garage. We clamber down to the beach with some chairs, light the fire and over the next couple of hours watch a spectacular sunset, flooding the sea with golden light.

We sit out late, until the tide is almost upon us, and we're forced to abandon the beach, feeling joy and sand swept pleasure to match that of any summer's day. Shattered, in the best possible way, we fall into bed and we're soon soundly asleep.

# Day 26: 15th October

Arisaig is beautiful this morning. It's one of the prettiest places I have ever visited in my life, and the wildlife isn't bad either. While I'm sitting working, enjoying the view, Stuart calls me to say there's a sea eagle flying over, so there's another thing off the list.

Mid-morning, we head out for a walk with the camera and Stuart catches curlew and other marine birds with the long lens. We were hoping to see sea otters here, and they are well documented in the area, but we're not lucky enough to see any today.

The walk is lovely, and the weather so good for the lateness of the season. As we wander along the beach, we discuss plans for the final few days of our trip.

The Fort William area is the next natural step. We are hoping to climb Ben Nevis this trip and we're carefully watching the mountain weather, as snow is starting to fall at the peaks. We had a late night out with the fire last night and we're both tired so we decide we'll drive towards Glen Nevis, write today off as an admin day and go and find somewhere quiet to do some laundry and empty our toilet.

When we get back to the van, we make some hot wraps for lunch, then sit and work out where the nearest laundry is between here and Fort William. There's a Revolution Laundry at Glen Nevis Holiday Park and the Internet says there's a drop in service for campervans so thinking that'll serve all our needs we head there.

The drive is beautiful enough to render one speechless, and as we get towards the biggest of Scotland's munro in this area, the weather, which has felt like late summer the last couple of days, gives way to more wintery vibes with visible snow and stratus clouds at the peaks.

We get to the holiday park, right in the shadow of Ben Nevis and the famous peaks that make up the Ring of Steal and have a chat to one of the staff about using the facilities.

The Revolution Laundry and all the motorhome services are in the centre of the park, so we put the washing on, then Stuart has a shower while I stay with the dog, catching up with work. While he's emptying the toilet, emptying our grey waste, and refilling the water, I grab a quick shower too.

The showers are lovely and clean, heated, and well-serviced. When we're in the van, we shower but we conserve water as we do so, always conscious that our supply isn't endless. Today, I shower in the huge cubicle, allowing the water to blast down on me, enjoying the pleasure of a plumbed system.

I have an extra long shower, wash my hair twice, pull on some leggings and a vest and exit the large cubicle, as I do I notice a row of urinals and in the split second it takes me to wonder why the ladies bathroom has urinals, the penny drops, and I hear two men walking into the bathroom. I dive into one of the toilet cubicles, giggling to myself, and end up having to stay there for ten minutes, hiding from the two male friends who are cheerfully chatting while performing their own ablutions. I finally get back to the van and regale the tale to Stuart, and sense much glee on his part. Never mind, at least I feel fresh and clean!

We're keeping a close eye on the weather, knowing that now there's snow on the peaks, we can only climb Ben Nevis if we get a window with good conditions. Tomorrow it's forecast to be snowing heavily on the peaks, so we decide we'll chase some waterfalls and plan two medium length hikes. Now we have a plan, and we're nice and clean with a full tank of water and an empty toilet and nice fresh bedding. Living the dream, baby!

There's no food in the van so it's next stop Morrisons where we pick up enough food to last the rest of the trip. We treat ourselves to some more beef olives, grab snacks aplenty for hiking. By the time we're finished, the day is almost over.

Our first walk tomorrow is for Inchree Falls so we make our way to the dedicated car park where we'll spend the night. It's still quite early so Stuart cooks while I get a few hours work done, then we settle down for the evening, ready for a busy today tomorrow.

## Day 27: 16th October

We're up and about and feeling refreshed after a couple of relaxing days. It's a murky day and when you look up, it's a white out on the peaks, indicating heavy snow is falling. We check the weather again for Nevis. Tomorrow is forecast to be a write-off of a day with the guarantee of rain every hour of the day but the Met Office forecast for Ben Nevis the day after is for a clear bright day. The big, and final plan is on! Two big waterfalls walks planned today, a relaxing day tomorrow, and then Nevis to finish the roadtrip with a bang!

We grab a quick breakfast, pack some stuff for the hike and get out, leaving the van at Inchree car park.

The trails here are easy to follow, leading us up through woodland where we stop and I take some pictures of the fairytale fly agaric growing here, and the tiny common bonnets, growing on the mossy twigs in this dense, damp woodland setting.

As we clear the wood towards the glen, we hear the falls before we see it, thunderous applause cheering us up the hillside towards it. There's a small viewing point, but we end up climbing down off the path for the best pictures.

This series of long drop falls is in full spate after the recent rainfall, and we stand a while marvelling at its power and discussing how deep its pools are, and how unpleasant it might be to find yourself in there tumbled about by the force of the water. The entire forest is wearing its warm coat and the scene is a glow of vibrant oranges, yellows, and reds.

We continue up through the woodland and have the most wonderful walk through the tall pine, finding mushrooms and enjoying the views over Fort William and its surrounding Munros and lochs.

As we walk along the trail we see a small waterfall just off the path and someone has built a tiny red model house next to the falls. It's the cutest scene, and we wonder if it mimics the scene at the big falls, although we did not see a house up there.

Finally, we start to drop down

through the forestry and back to the van, finishing the loop and completing our first hike of the day.

After some lunch it's off to the lower falls car park for the Steall waterfall walk. The car park here is huge with specific motorhome parking and a toilet in the car park. We get parked up and start up the track for the walk, coming almost immediately to a bridge over Lower Falls, water crashing all around the bridge, creating rainbows and showering us with spray.

We follow the trail up the gorge, taking in the views, from the waterfalls to the snowy peaks above us, it's breathtaking! We follow the forestry road for a while, cars occasionally passing us up to the higher car parks.

Eventually we get to the large falls at the Waters of Nevis, and the final car park. I stop to fill my water bottle in the falls, and we continue past the road's end. It's about here we realise we may have underestimated the length of the walk, and this is where most people probably park. However, every tiny bridge on this last section had a weight warning and it all felt a tad unsuitable for the van. It's our second hike of the day, we're around 3.5km in and we still have a couple of kilometres left before we get to the falls.

From here the track becomes a lot harder underfoot, following an eroded stone pathway along the water's edge, deep gorges, falls, and narrow ravines feature along the route.

A gorge appears to our right, full of huge boulders, narrowing the water to a torrent of white force. Naturally, we head over and hop a few boulders, taking pictures and enjoying nature's playground a little. We rejoin the path and continue along this rocky, narrow track, through waterfalls, along ledges, and clambering up well-worn stones.

Eventually the path flattens out, and with the river to our right we meander along the path, boggy ground to either side. Like many of Scotland's natural water features, we can hear Steall Falls before we get to it. A cacophony of noise in the distance alerting us of its proximity.

The waterfall is on the other side of the river with access only via the Glen Nevis Rope Bridge. We were aware that this was here, and that in all possibilities we were not going to be able to cross with the dog, but there's a great view of the falls even from across the river.

Just for fun, Stuart climbs and crosses via the rope bridge, a crossing made up of three strong, steel wires and frame to make up a precarious bridge. I have a go myself but I'm short and I struggle to stretch my arms to hold onto the ropes either side of me. I'm usually a bit of a daredevil but this one beat me and I clamber down. We hang around for a while, Stuart puts the drone up, and then we retrace our steps back to the van. It's been a long day!

We get back to the car park late, hungry, and keen to find somewhere to settle down for the evening. I use the car park toilet and again marvel at the clever composting systems they have in these remote places.

It's late in the day and we've made the rookie mistake of not pre-arranging our park up. We usually plan ahead, but Scotland has been so good to us we've been lulled into a false sense of security. Fort William is a very busy place and as we drive, the best we see is paid motorhome parking, but it's 6 metres maximum. At 7.5 metres long we might have a problem!

We're both hungry and ready to call it a day so I check the apps and maps and find a few park ups dotted on the Old Military Road above Fort William. We make our way in that direction with just two requirements, flat enough to sleep, and with Internet. It's really getting late now, and as we drive past each park up on the map it's either already home to a couple of vans, or it's an Internet dead spot. We drive almost three miles before we find an empty spot and it's easy to see why it's empty. I'm sure this is the only layby ever to be classified a hill. I only wish I was exaggerating.

Stuart does a bit of reversing back and fore, and pops the van up on some chocks, which makes no noticeable difference at all, and we have some dinner and sleep on such a slope that every time we wake up in the night, we're halfway down the bed. It's the closest to sleeping standing up I've ever done.

# Day 28: 17th October

I wake up to the sound of animals and lie there a little while trying to work out if it's a stag or a cow, I decide on cow and quite quickly after that decide to get up, as I'm already half standing anyway. I think that's the least flat park up we've ever used and rather than stay here, living on a slope, we decide to head off immediately and find somewhere a bit flatter to spend the day.

To use the correct terminology, it's a dreich day, and we're tired after yesterday. The forecast looks good for climbing Ben Nevis tomorrow so today is a rest day for us, and a work day for me. We drive back down the Old Military Road a little towards town and come to the Blarmacfoldach viewpoint. We can't see a thing; visibility is at less than 20 metres with the rain but it's flat and the signal is good, so we pull over and I pop the kettle on.

There's a bench here and a small area to sit and take in the view. As views go, visibility is at a minimum, but once it clears it's a beautiful view of the now snow-capped Ben Nevis, and a vantage point over the whole of Fort William. Even with the gloomy weather, it's hard to deny its beauty. Beautiful but fierce, and as I'm looking up at the snow on Ben Nevis it has me feeling a little nervous for tomorrow. I resolve to check my pack and waterproof my shell later ready for the walk.

There's a small tent pitched up on the grassy area in front of the van, and after a few hours we both start to wonder if the person inside is ok. It's the kind of tent you pack up and walk with, rather than leave to explore. The weather has been awful and it's no better today so Stuart pops over to check and finds a young Dutch guy who is fine, if a little wet through. They chat for a while, leaving me to finish up work, then it's time to check our kit and waterproof our gear ready for tomorrow.

So far, our usually adequate hiking gear has proven no match for the worst of the Scottish days, driving us back on a couple of Munros. None of us want that tomorrow so instead of using the waterproofing spray, we decide to use the paint on version of Fabsil, usually reserved for tents and pop tops. Stuart decides I should wear my coat to make it easier to paint the waterproofer on and much hilarity ensues, I suspect much aided by the chemicals in the Fabsil! I'm positive I'm utterly waterproofed by the time we've finished, right down to my skin, so I return the favour and hopefully we're all ready to add Ben Nevis to our mountain bagging list.

Once we're all organised we decide to head off and settle down for an early night ready for Ben Nevis tomorrow.

We're going to walk from the Achintee Road Car Park near the Ben Nevis Inn and all indications are you can stay the night. The damp, dull day has turned into heavy rain, it seems hard to believe tomorrow's forecast is so good.

As we pull off and head down the road we very quickly come alongside the young man from the tent, he's soaked through with all his gear hanging off him.

We pull over and ask him where he's going, he's off to the Ben Nevis Youth Hostel, also with the plan of climbing Nevis tomorrow. We have no belted seats in the back but there's a bench and it's only a couple of miles, so we offer him a lift, for which he is grateful.

We drive through town, chatting away with our new found friend who has come here to start a new job but has taken a few days in Scotland as a treat. It's rained for his whole time here so let's hope for some sun tomorrow, for him as well as us. As we get closer to the car park, Stuart misjudges his speed over a speed bump. The van is long, which means it has a fair bit of bounce at the rear end, he sends the poor lad flying for the ceiling, setting us all off in fits of laughter.

We drop him off, he's eager to get to the Youth Hostel and dry out his kit and clothes, then we park up for the evening. The spaces are tight and lots of people are parked alongside each other, us included. But there's enough room for our long van, and we're grateful we got here early as by sunset almost every spot is taken.

Stuart cooks a quick meal of chicken and bacon wraps, one of our van favourites and we settle down for an early night, rucksacks packed, and the alarm set for a little before sunrise.

## Day 29: 18th October

It's still dark when we wake, not a hint of dawn, we're up before the sun! It's forecast to feel like -8 at the peak so I pull on a base layer and get into my hiking gear, shovel down a big bowl of muesli and fruit and I'm raring to go!

The forecast was for a bright, clear day but as we head out for a day's walking it's damp with mist and low cloud. What a horrible day. I really hope we make it to the peak, at this stage the chance of a view is a distant dream.

The estimated walk time is 7-8 hours for this walk so I'm hoping the early morning mist will lift, let's see how things pan out.

At the end of the car park, a sign directs us to the path, which starts to rise almost immediately, and we soon rise above the glen, invisible in the mist. We cross narrow bridges and make our way along the narrow path, climbing all the time until suddenly the sun is on our faces as we get above the mist in the valley.

The skies, blue above us, the glen, filled with mist beneath us, it really is a wondrous sight, and we stop a while, catch our breath, and enjoy the spectacular cloud inversion. I've been climbing mountains for years now and I have never seen a cloud inversion, so to experience my first while climbing Ben Nevis is a treat!

We get on our way again and eventually the path curves to the left, revealing more hills, more valleys, and even more magical inversions, putting us above the cloud. Eventually we rise so high it looks as though the whole of Scotland's lowlands are sitting in mist beneath us as we look down from our sunny vantage point.

As climbs go, so far Ben Nevis is steady, gradual, and really only requires being able to keep putting one foot in front of the other for eight hours. We'll see how it gets further up. We reach the Red Burn, the accepted halfway point in two and a half hours, which means the whole walk is likely to take us around eight, which is what we expected. We're the kind of people who stop for a view to take pictures and like to stop often to enjoy the scenery… and snacks.

There's been a lot of rain and the Red Burn is a bit of a challenge. This burn tumbles down the side of Nevis, easily two metres wide, and it must be crossed to continue to the summit. We watch a few people, each with their own methods of crossing as we decide a route for ourselves that will keep our feet as dry as possible. In the end I opt for the "run for it" method and hop from rock to rock on momentum alone, and Stuart lets the dog come through to me before he hops across after me.

A little way along the path we sit on a large rock for a snack and a quick cereal bar turns into a chat with some other walkers, and a twenty-minute social. The day is stunning and everyone is in good spirits at the half way point. A short way after the Red Burn, the famous zigzags start along the rocky ascent up this collapsed volcano. With the zigzags come the first snow, and Nala, who loves the white stuff, amuses everyone by rolling and wriggling around in it.

Bit by bit we chip away at the climb, the last section steep, snowy and slippery underfoot. It's been a long hike, elevation with every step. We meander through the cairns, here to guide walkers in bad weather, preventing them falling into the treacherous Five-Finger Gully, and finally come out onto the top of the mountain.

 The day is perfect, and it's hard to describe how beautiful it is up here.

I'm a little taken aback by just how many buildings and erections are up here, a stone cairn, a trig on a stone tower, a meteorological station, with connected hut, and a stone plinth with a plaque about the station. It's the most manmade stonework I've ever seen on a hill, which surprises me on the biggest hill in Great Britain.

As is usually the case, everyone is jovial and chatty, celebrating reaching the top, making conversation and basking in the moment. We take some pictures and Stuart puts the drone up, getting some fantastic footage of us on the peak.

It's so snowy, I keep sinking, knee deep between rocks as it's impossible to see what the terrain is underneath the snow. We walk to the edge, and after the earlier inversion, we see a fog bow, the first one I have ever seen.

Stuart walks out to the rocky edge and calls me over, and we add a Brocken spectre to the list of mountain firsts we've ticked off today, our shadow, perfectly encased in a radial rainbow, the sun at our backs, and clouds beneath us. I don't know how to explain just how perfect today has been, and to then be treated to every mountain phenomenon you can imagine too, is unbelievable.

We're about an hour on the top, and absolutely freezing by the time we decide to descend. Back we go along the route we followed up, retracing our steps down the mountain.

The icy steep at the top is challenging to descend, but we get down in one piece, the entire day coming in at about eight and a half hours.

We're exhausted, but we did it, we climbed Nevis, and we had the most perfect conditions we could hope for.

Both of us are absolutely ravenous but neither of us wants to cook so we look up local takeaways and make our way back into Fort William where we buy a feast for at least six people from the China Palace takeaway.

We stop at the waterfront car park and eat it straight out of the cartons in the cab, watching a group of wild swimming ladies brave the cold water with little inhibition, and enjoy a lovely sunset across the water.

Our trip is almost over, and we've now decided which day we're heading home. The only area we have now not covered is Glencoe, so in the hope of getting a full day's exploring in there tomorrow (no rest for the wicked!), we make our way to a place called Seagull Island where we've spotted a potentially beautiful park up by the loch. As we approach, a stag appears along the road to the left, causing us to brake hard, no harm done.

It's dark when we arrive at the park up, never a bad thing, as it usually means you wake up to a nice surprise. We call it a day and hit the sack, exhausted.

## Day 30: 19th October

It's 10:45am when I wake up, I am alone in the van with the dog. I pull back the blinds on Stuart's side of the bed to be greeted by the most beautiful loch side view. The Autumn colours are dazzling, the loch reflecting the greens, yellows, oranges, and ochre shades. The mountains of Glencoe visible at the other end of the water.

I can see Stuart by the lake, he's up and about already and he's gone out to look at the view. Who can blame him? I put my oversized hoodie on and go to the door and call him, he looks back with a huge, knowing grin. We've woken up in paradise... again!

Don't let anyone tell you Scotland is just another British holiday, it's been the trip of a lifetime, and to be able to spend an entire month in this beautiful country has been an utter privilege for both of us.

That said, we're exhausted, and I am not up for any big hikes today. After several coffees and a chat, we decide to do the traditional 'road trip' thing and take a scenic drive through Glencoe, a friend recommends we visit Glen Etive so we add that to the list too. I make another coffee for the road; we have a late breakfast and head towards Glencoe.

The roads are busy, and since we arrived at Fort William it's felt a lot more touristy than the first part of our trip. The people aren't too much of a distraction though as this area oozes eye-popping beauty. Lush green lowlands surround us, with waterfalls, rivers and glens in every direction, rising up to autumnal bracken, glowing gold on the hills until they give way to craggy, sharp, protuberances as old as the universe itself, reaching up to the skies.

The road follows the river, and we watch the kayakers navigate the river in spate after all the recent rain, pull over to take some photos, and generally enjoy our meander through the mountains, even spotting Jimmy Saville's dilapidated cottage (You can't miss it, it's full of graffiti!).

Eventually we see the turning for Glen Etive. This road doesn't lead anywhere and comes to a dead end at Loch Etive but we're promised a scenic drive and the it's time for a dog walk so we meander through the mountains, taking in the views.

We haven't gone very far when we see a stag on the side of the road, we pull over and realise the field too is full of hinds and several other stag. Nala is fixated on the one closest to the van, watching it, eyes wide. We stop a while and watch them before continuing down the road.

It's several miles to Loch Etive and we arrive just in time as within half an hour the small car park is full. There's a family camped up on the shores, cooking lunch outside in front of two tents they have set up. We leave the van and walk a while along the shore, glad to have the chance to stretch our legs after the drive. It's beautiful here, the rocky shore littered with impossibly large boulders that I ended up climbing for fun, mountains disappearing into the clouds all around us.

By the time we get back to the van, it's incredibly busy here, two VW T4s are waiting to enter the car park, and there's another van behind that trying to get in. We make haste and hop in the van, drive a couple of miles up the road and find a scenic somewhere to pull over to make lunch.

Stuart takes the drone and flies it towards Buachaille Etive Mòr, getting some cracking shots of the surrounding countryside, and the van, and then we tuck into scrambled eggs and baguettes before we decide what to do with the rest of our final day.

This area has been a treat for the eyes, and we should have really offered it more than a day of our trip. We earmark it to come back in the future and make plans to get on.

We want to continue heading South so we add Kilchurn Castle to the stops and hit the road again, arriving at the car park a little while later. From the car park, Stuart spots a bird of prey in the distance, we watch it a while and agree it's probably a sea eagle, before we take the short walk – through a herd of huge cows spread across the path – down the path to the castle.

Sadly the castle is fenced off due to falling masonry but we have a nice walk around, look at the loch, and have a little look around the woodland here for mushrooms, then make our way back to the van for our final stop today at the Falls of Falloch. We're about to dip back into the Loch Lomond and the Trossachs area, which attentive readers will realise means we've gone full circle in thirty days!

We had the Falls of Falloch pinned as one of the things to do on the way up but never got around to it. There's been a lot of rain so we're hoping for a treat today. We swing into the car park, which thankfully isn't very busy then make our way down to the falls, following the deep, thundering roar.

The falls are breathtaking, and we walk down to the rocky river's edge to appreciate them. A cascade of water, gushes from the hillside, framed by the orange and yellow hues of Autumn. We're on the edge of the river, but we can see a viewing platform to our left, so we walk over. The platform takes the form of a long cage tunnel, oxidised and aged in the weather so its rusty surface blends into the surrounding landscape. At the end, a poem about the falls is cut into the metal platform, offering a perfect view of the falls from a safe platform. After taking some pictures, we continue on our way, meandering South as we go.

We've seen endless waterfalls during this trip, large crashing ones, long drop ones, meandering ones, and ephemeral ones, and at no point have I got in the slightest bit sick of looking at them. Scotland, you have been glorious!

We find a park up at Loch Lomond at Milarrochy Bay that looks promising, so we make our way there for our final night. It's dark when we arrive, and raining, it's also forecast to rain for the whole next day. We really want to visit the Devil's Pulpit just outside Glasgow as our final walk, but we'll see. We fall into bed exhausted, hoping for a change in the weather for our last day. We've been quite lucky so far, so who knows!

## Day 31: 20th October

We're awake early as the rain on the roof is so loud! We really wanted to bring you the happiest of endings to this story, but today is not the day for a gorge walk! We cancel our final plan, and mentally prepare for the long drive home. After some breakfast, we walk with the dog along the shoreline while the rain beats down on us. When we get back to the van, Stuart reorganises some bits while I play with the dog at the shore. I take one picture of her by the lone tree in the water in the bay, the last picture I will take in Scotland, and then we start the long drive home.

Thank you, Scotland, for the trip of a lifetime, you were wonderful!

Until the next adventure…
Dare to dream!

# The Interactive Route

Scan the QR code with your phone's camera for the interactive route with what3word locations for every stop off (what3words.com)

# Quick Itinerary

### DAY 1: PENRITH

- Overnight stop at the base of the Beacon Hill Monument, near Penrith (Free. Flat parking area)

### DAY 2: BEACON HILL MONUMENT, GARELOCH, GARE LOCH

- Beacon Hill Monument walk
- Walk along the trail to Gare Loch
- Back to the van for an overnight stop at Whistlefield Car Park (Free. Flat car park with many spaces)

### DAY 3: SUCCOTH, THE COBBLER HIKE, LOCH ECK

- Succoth Car Park (Pay and Display, £1ph, no overnight signs)
- The Cobbler hike (11km, strenuous hike)
- Loch Eck (East shore) for an overnight park up (free, but camping permits required in season for Loch Lomond and the Trossachs)

### DAY 4: LOCH ECK, PUCK'S GLEN, LOCH EARN

- Loch Eck (East shore) for an overnight park up (free, but camping permits may be required in season for this area)
- Puck's Glen and Big Trees Trail hike (5km, moderate)
- Loch Earn at the foot of Ben Vorlich for an overnight park up (free, but camping permits may be required in season for this area)

### DAY 5: LOCH EARN, BEN VORLICH HIKE

- Ben Vorlich hike (13km, strenuous)
- Loch Earn for an overnight park up (free, but camping permits may be required in season for this area)

### DAY 6: PERTH, THE HERMITAGE

- Tesco Superstore, Perth (groceries and fuel stop)
- The Hermitage/Ossian's Hall trail (8km, moderate)
- Small car park between the Old Military Road/Inver Mill caravan park for overnight park up (free, but no overnighting signs)

### DAY 7: A'CHAILEACH HIKE, NEWTONMORE

- A' Chaileach, Cairngorms (9km there and back, strenuous)
- Newtonmore, Glen Road. (free, roadside parking on mountain track)

### DAY 8: RUTHVEN BARRACKS, FALLS OF FOYER, LOCH NESS

- Ruthven Barracks
- The Falls of Foyers
- Loch Ness Layby, General Wade's Military Road (free parking on side of road)

### DAY 9: LAUNDRY, ROSEMARKIE, CHANONRY POINT, BRORA BEACH

- Revolution Laundry, Esso fuel station at the Muir of Ord
- Rosemarkie
- Chanonry Point
- The Bear's Den, Brora (cracking fish and chips!)
- Brora Beach car park for overnight stay (free, beachside parking)

### DAY 10: FORSINARD TOWER, FORSINAIN TRAIL, SANDSIDE BAY BEACH

- Forsinard Tower and Forsinard Flows Nature Reserve (A897)
- Forsinain Trail walk (park up on A897 near logging hut)
- Sandside Bay Beach (free, but with no overnighting signs)

### DAY 11: JOHN O'GROATS, DUNCANSBY STACKS, DUNNET HEAD, CASTLETOWN BEACH

- John O' Groats (large car park)
- Duncansby Stacks (short walk from large car park)
- Dunnet Head (clifftop parking)
- Castletown Beach for overnight stay (small free, beachside car park)

### DAY 12: ACHININVER BEACH, MOINE HOUSE

- Castletown Beach swim
- Achininver Beach (parking for one or two vehicles, no charge)
- Moine House parking off the A838 for overnight stay (Small, flat parking area, no charge)

## DAY 13: CEANNABEINNE BEACH, SMOO CAVE, BALNAKEIL BEACH, KYLE OF DURNESS

- Ceannabeinne Beach (car park above beach, free)
- Smoo Cave
- Balnakeil Beach (flat car park and bins, no overnighting signs)
- Kyle of Durness, Stories in Sand car park (free flat car park, very exposed)

## DAY 14: BALNAKEIL BEACH, SMOO CAVE, CULKEIN ROAD

- Balnakeil Beach hike (free parking at Balnakeil House)
- Smoo Cave (Revolution Laundry and overnight pay and display car park)
- Culkein Road (small pull in on side of road, very windy, not recommended)

## DAY 15: STOER LIGHTHOUSE, LITTLE ASSYNT, ARDVECK CASTLE, ULLAPOOL

- Stoer Lighthouse (flat, exposed car park facing the sea, free)
- Old Man of Stoer Hike
- Little Assynt Car Park (free, flat car park on side of the A837)
- Ardveck Castle
- Layby on A835 into Ullapool (free, set back from road)

## DAY 16: CORRISHALLOCH GORGE, ARDESSIE FALLS, LITTLE LOCH BROOM

- Corrieshalloch Gorge National Nature Reserve
- Ardessie Falls
- Overnight stay overlooking Little Loch Broom just off the A832 (free, with picnic tables and bins)

### DAY 17: GAIRLOCH BEACH, GAIRLOCH HARBOUR, APPLECROSS SANDS

· Gairloch Beach Car Park for beach (free flat car park, no overnighting)
· Gairloch Harbour (toilets, CDP, Grey water disposal, fresh drinking water (donation recommended)
· Victoria Falls in Achnasheen (flat, free gravel car park off road)
· Applecross Sands (free gravel car park at beach on the edge of military land)

### DAY 18: APPLECROSS PASS, BHEINN BHAN, PLOCKTON AIRFIELD

- Applecross Pass/ Bealach na Ba (not to be underestimated in large vehicles)
- Beinn Bhan hike (9km, strenuous)
- Off the Croft takeaway (Plockton)
- Park up alongside Plockton Airfield (free, flat with bins, alongside the sea)

### DAY 19: PLOCKTON CORAL BEACH, SLIGACHAN OLD BRIDGE, EAS A 'BHRADAIN FALLS, RIGG VIEWPOINT

· Plockton Coral Beach (less than 1km walk from the airfield)
· Co-op, Kyle of Lochalsh
· River walk from Sligachan Old Bridge (Parked at the Sligachan Hotel, free)
· Eas a 'Bhradain falls (layby just past the falls)
· Rigg Viewpoint (disused track just off A87 near Storr, sea views)

### DAY 20: TALISKER DISTILLERY, EYENORT RIVER

- Gleaner fuel, Uig , Uig harbour (public toilets here)
- Talisker Distillery (large car park with toilets and showers nearby with pay machines)
- Overnight stop at the Eyenort River small parking area. (Take second left out of Carbost on the B8009, about half a mile along on the right)

## DAY 21: OLD MAN OF STORR, KILT ROCK, MEALT FALLS, AN CORRAN BEACH

- Old Man of Storr (Pay and Display car park, with toilets also paid)
- Kilt Rock and Mealt Falls viewpoint (Free car park, short walk to feature)
- An Corran Beach (Free parking alongside the beach)

## DAY 22: UIG, THE FAIRY GLEN, LOCH SCAVAIG

- Gleaner Fuel, Uig (public toilets at harbour)
- The Fairy Glen (pay and display parking on roadside)
- Co-op Portree
- Loch Scavaig (Parking at Elgol Beach, no signal)
- Roadside parking on B8083 (small area to pull in off road)

## DAY 23: BLA BHEINN HIKE, RIGG VIEWPOINT

- Bla Bheinn Hike (12km strenuous hike over difficult terrain. Flat, large car park, free)
- Rigg Viewpoint (disused track just off A87 near Storr, sea views)

## DAY 24: QUIRAING, PLOCKTON

- Quiraing (Pay and display parking, no overnight)
- Off the Croft Takeaway (Plockton)
- Park up alongside Plockton Airfield (free, flat with bins, alongside the sea)

### DAY 25: CAMUSDARACH BEACH, ARISAIG

- Camusdarach Beach
- Traigh Beach, Arisaig (roadside) (Arisaig is very small with few park ups and we recommend a campsite)

### DAY 26: ARISAIG, GLEN NEVIS HOLIDAY PARK, INCHREE FALLS

- Glen Nevis Holiday Park and Revolution Laundry (£10 for campervan service, plus laundry fee)
- Morrisons, Aird Road, Fort William
- Inchree Falls Car Park (waterfall car park, free)

### DAY 27: INCHREE FALLS, STEALL WATERFALLS

- Inchree Falls circular walk (4-5km)
- Steall Waterfall walk (10km)
- Old Military Road (Lots of laybys and park ups, get there early)

### DAY 28: BLARMACFOLDACH VIEWPOINT, ACHINTEE ROAD

- Blarmacfoldach viewpoint (flat, scenic area on the Old Military Road)
- Achintee Road Car Park (free car park near the Ben Nevis Inn, limited spaces)

### DAY 29: BEN NEVIS, SEAGULL ISLAND

- Ben Nevis (Mountain Track route from Achintee Road Car Park)
- China Palace, 155 High St, Fort William PH33 6EA
- West End Car Park (loch side parking)
- Seagull Island Viewpoint, Kinlochleven (free, overnight parking at the loch side)

### DAY 30: GLENCOE, GLEN ETIVE, KILCHURN CASTLE, FALLS OF FALLOCH, MILARROCHY BAY

- Scenic drive through Glencoe and Glen Etive.
- Loch Etive (small car park alongside the lake)
- Kilchurn Castle (large free car park, short walk to castle)
- Falls of Falloch (small free car park on a slope)
- Milarrochy Bay (overnight, no charge out of season, camping permits required in summer. Toilets available)

**BONUS TRACKS**

### Day 10 Update by Kath

The one where I summarise the first ten days of the trip and how we've found Scotland to date

### Nala does the twist

The one where Nala comes a cropper trying to get a drink at the Forsinand trail on day 10 of our trip.

### Scotland by Nala

The one where you see the whole Scottish road trip from the perspective of Nala, our lurcher

### Scotland: The Pictures

The one where you get to see the best of the rest of the pictures we couldn't fit in this book.

# The Hills and Hikes

If a hike is listed in the itinerary but not listed here then expect a well signposted trail that is easy to follow. For the hills and Munros, scan the QR codes to load the routes we took. If you are using the Ordnance Survey app, routes will open in the app, if not, you'll receive the route in your browser. Be aware, many Munros are low signal areas, so maps need to be downloaded/printed before you set out.

We consider ourselves to be experienced hikers, who bagged over a hundred peaks last year. Please take care and stay within your own capabilities when hiking. Ensure you are prepared, check the weather forecast and take some navigational aids with you.

### DAY 3: THE COBBLER

An 11km, strenuous hike with some scrambling and climbing. Those who don't wish to scramble can ascend up our descent route where there is a clearer path to the peak.

### DAY 5: BEN VORLICH

A 14km, strenuous hike. Our route took us down across low land, but it was boggy and we don't recommend it so we've just provided a there and back route.

### DAY 7: A'CHAILLEACH, CAIRNGORMS

A 10km, strenuous there and back hike over boggy ground. A bothy offers some shelter before the prominence of the hill.

### DAY 18: BEINN BHAN

A 11km, strenuous there and back hike over boggy ground with no discernible paths and some small scrambles.

### DAY 23: BLA BHEINN

10km, strenuous, technical hike over scree and boulders with scrambles and challenging descents into wet gullies.

### DAY 29: BEN NEVIS

18km, strenuous hike up Britain's biggest mountain. Not advised during winter. This walk involves over 1300 metres of elevation.

# ROUTE

| LOCATION | DATE |
|---|---|
|  |  |

# ROUTE

| LOCATION | DATE |
|---|---|
|  |  |

# ROUTE

| LOCATION | DATE |
|---|---|
|  |  |